N04 3·95

1-00

BEGINNER'S GUIDE TO TROPICAL FISH
(Fish tanks, Coldwater aquarium fish, Pond fish, Ponds and Marines)

BEGINNER'S GUIDE TO TROPICAL FISH

(Fish tanks, Coldwater aquarium fish, Pond fish, Ponds and Marines)

Reginald Dutta BA FZS

PELHAM BOOKS

First published in Great Britain by
PELHAM BOOKS LTD
44 Bedford Square
London WC1B 3DP
1971
Reprinted 1971, 1975, 1976
New Edition 1984
Reprinted 1985

British Library Cataloguing in Publication Data

Dutta, Reginald
    Beginner's guide to tropical fish.—2nd ed.
    1. Tropical fish
    I. Title
    639.3'4   SF457

ISBN 0 7207 1506 7

Printed lithographically in Great Britain
by Hollen Street Press Ltd, at Slough
and bound by
Hunter & Foulis Ltd,
Edinburgh

To the Staff, Fish, and Customers of
Fish Tanks Ltd, without whose co-operation
this knowledge might never have been gained.

Contents

CONTENTS

Illustrations
(between pages 76 and 77)

ROSY BARBS

TIGER BARBS

BLACK WIDOW

DWARF GOURAMI

PEARL GOURAMI

HARLEQUIN FISH

KUHLI LOACH

PENGUIN FISH

PLATIES

P. PLECOSTOMUS

ZEBRA DANIOS

PTEROPHYLLUM SCALARE

SCATOPHAGUS ARGUS

BARBUS SCHUBERTI

CHILODUS PUNCTATUS

The author and publishers gratefully acknowledge permission to use the photographs of Laurence E. Perkins

Line drawings by Olive Dutta.

CHAPTER ONE

IT'S THE FISH THAT COUNTS

Let's get first things right first. Who is the most important one concerned with the fish tank? Clearly it's not you. It's the fish. For the fish tank is its whole home and its whole life, twenty-four hours of each and every day, no change, no holiday, no escape. Only a heartless selfish brute could fail to register that, on reflection; a kindly human would cease at once such talk as 'it's only to amuse the kids, or just to fill in that space' — who but a cruel tyrant would sacrifice fish life and happiness 'just to amuse someone or to fulfil some whim'!

So, it's the fish that counts.

Fortunately fish are very accommodating creatures and are only too anxious to co-operate, to please, to take on your habits and to do all they can to make you glad. They just ask to live, decently if possible; happily if also possible; then they will offer you years of friendship and adoration in return. They will come when you call or when you approach the fish tank; they will listen to your voice, flapping excited fins in response, all to a degree that you won't believe till you've had your own fish tank for a month or so and have personally verified these truths.

And if you now think that fish have no feelings, have no psychic rapport with you, can't hear your voice or feel your presence, then they'll soon teach you the contrary. That's why they make such good pets. Added to which they demand very little of your time or attention in return *provided* that you have set up their home with knowledge and skill, as well as understanding; in other words, that you have bought your tank from a specialist dealer who really knows his job and can put you on the right lines from the word go. A 'pet shop' dealer has little hope of keeping abreast with this rapidly changing, fast-growing industry if his attention is spread over dogs, cats or whatever; he *has* to concentrate only and solely on fish. A general knowledge of mammals is no more applicable to tropical fish than is a general knowledge of clothes to choosing an expensive fur coat, or a general knowledge of motor-cars to making an orbiting missile. You need a specialist, a true expert, one who gives all his time, energy and resources to fish alone.

CHAPTER TWO

CREATING A HOME
FIT FOR THE FISH

Again, first things first — the home should be big enough; fish suffer and die in cramped conditions just like you and I would. So please get the very largest tank that is practicable. Other furnishings and fittings can always be added later, as and when possible; but, once bought, the tank can't be enlarged. The air surface of the prospective new tank is the real key, rather than mere volume of water, as its area controls the rate at which the good gases like oxygen can come into the water and the bad gases like carbon dioxide can escape out. Fouling, decay, smells and disease become increasingly liable as the area of the air surface becomes smaller; beware of the plausible dealer who says it will be all right if you have air bubbles from a small pump; these bubbles will certainly help, but will they help enough! Tanks with a small air surface usually need sophisticated filters that probably cost as much as the money 'saved' by getting a tank whose air surface was too small.

Specialist tanks are constantly coming into the shops for sale and many are most beautiful and original in design; but they should all conform to Mother Nature's basic law of an ample air surface, and the customer who ignores this gets the troubles he deserves, not to mention the poor fish who suffer and die.

Fabulous is about the only word to describe the choice of tanks now available. Still going strong are the lightweight pressed steel frames glazed with thin glass; cheap to buy and quick to leak the public loves them and they are sold in thousands of pet shops over five continents. At one time it looked as though the trouble with leaks would finally cause them to be replaced by better versions but improved sealing glues have prolonged their usefulness, and many a small child has pestered many a harassed parent into buying one — as it is so cheap.

The more robust, more reliable, strong angle-iron framed tank is starting to fade as a favourite. Again, very inexpensive, it too is widely sold and looks like so continuing for decades to come. It used to rust, but the nylon coatings, and polythene coatings of the angle-iron have cured that. It used to leak, especially if emptied and moved, but the new liquid rubber sealers have cured that too. It's a good old familiar friend, and survives.

These new liquid rubberised sealers are an important technical break-through. Before their advent the angle-iron had to be wide enough to allow sufficient waterproofing; dealers used to (and still do) skimp on this width resulting in greater leaks but in cheaper tanks; now the new sealers will join glass to glass, eliminating the angle-iron altogether if required. Thus have grown up a whole generation of new type tanks: on the one hand all-glass completely frameless versions; on the other, many lovely metals previously not robust enough to allow adequate sealing but now being increasingly used — stainless steel, plastic strips and anodised aluminium to mention but three. More and more popular is becoming the custom of mixing materials in previously unheard of combinations: glass with wood, with plastics and resins of all kinds, as well as with metals. Such tanks can be very very beautiful and original, or even just be cheap and functional.

Of course, the biggest single change has come from the plastic industry as this now gears up to stamp out in-oneunbroken-piece tanks of useful depths and widths; years ago, a few centimetres was all the depth that was readily available, but as that has changed a stream of specialist plastic tanks descends on a delighted public which cannot but help marvel at the originality, variety, beauty, and colours of this fascinating new media — especially the colours. Plastics have the endearing quality of catching the light and of allowing it to travel through their slightly etherical form, to give intriguing and ever-changing hues. Add to colour two other big advantages of plastics, namely curves and fluting; these can be designed to give works of sheer beauty quite impossible with the more rigid and older-fashioned materials. And, to top it all, plastic tanks are light in weight — an important point in these modern days of air travel.

Rectangular tanks to go along a wall, on a shelf or a table; triangular ones to fit snugly into a corner though at the serious sacrifice of air-surface and hence of fish capacity; square or multi-sided ones that you can walk right round, can incorporate into a decor for your table or for circular seating; tanks encased in wood or in plastic cabinets, rather like TV sets; bowl-shaped tanks in single or in multiple units, with or without decorative stands; tanks with sloping fronts, sloping sides, coming forward or receding back; curved fronts, convex or concave; combinations of all these — fantastic choices. You can have a truly one-off job made by a specialist firm, the only single one in existence, just specially for that spot in that room, in that decor, in that shape, in that exact finish; to look gorgeous!

If you have a boat or a yacht and you want tanks to house decorative (or even edible) fish, this can also be done. Long since solved are design difficulties of equalising pressures and partial vacuum as the ship pitches and rolls, and the tank water surges and falls.

15

More humdrum but very useful tanks for breeding, for isolation; tanks divided into two or more parts; all now are readily available from your specialist dealer. The pet shop man might have just sold you a 'tank divider', often a piece of plastic inserted snugly into the tank to separate one portion from another, and have let it go at that; a specialist dealer would probably have warned you that perforating the plastic may not ensure an even distribution of heat in the separated parts, and may thus have saved you many a future (unnecessary) headache.

Tank position
Now that you have bought your (big-an-air-surface-as-possible) tank, where are you going to position it? Too much light, especially sunlight, means that the water will tend to grow green unless you have truly adequate filters, which are fortunately readily available. Too many fumes from a kitchen and a bathroom, for example, would also call for a change of site, or a filter. Too near a window would tend to induce greater temperature fluctuations as the outside climate changes, and would call for a stronger heating unit. Padding, between the tank and the window glass, would be a sensible precaution. Even a simple piece of hardboard would help, and would also cut excess light if it were higher and longer than the tank itself.

Then, where are you going to sit? You may now think this is a silly question, but when you have become entranced by your tank, a powerfully riveting focus for you and your friends, you'll find yourself shifting furniture around so that you can sit the more frontally and nearer the tank! If circumstances force you to remain far away, then have a few bigger fish in a bigger tank, rather than numerous small ones not so readily viewed from a distance, to save your constantly going

16

over to peer at the fascinating colours and antics.

To save constant backache and osteopath fees, please put the tank at a sensible height off the ground. Ideally, its *base* should be 90cm (36in) up from the floor for sitting eye-level, and 120cm (48in) for places like a hall-way or corridor where you are normally standing or walking. Tropical fish especially, lose far too much of their beauty if looked at from above; they should be at eye-level, or above. This point is important, and is not always realised at the beginning; many a lovely tank has been placed too low down 'because the furniture is modern' or the architect said so, and then has had to be raised to eye-level again.

Stands

When full of water, sand and the decorative rocks the tank can be heavy, so that any stand needs to be robust. As a rough guide a 45cm × 30cm × 30cm (18in × 12in × 12in) filled tank would weigh 38kg ($\frac{3}{4}$ cwt); a 60cm × 30cm × 30cm (24in × 12in × 12in) about 38kg to 50kg ($\frac{3}{4}$ to 1 cwt); and a 90cm × 30cm × 30cm (36in × 12in × 12in) tank, 100kg (2 cwt); although these are static weights, there is no jolting or movement, and so they are evenly distributed over the tank base area, so they are not quite as frightening as they first appear.

To repeat, other trends notwithstanding, the ideal height of the stand for sitting eye level is 90cm (36in) for optimum fish beauty, and 120cm (48in) for standing viewing.

Many and various are the types available. The stand of metal angle-iron is still deservedly popular because it is functional and very cheap, often it has a second metal frame support lower down which can house an additional tank or hold simply a glass shelf for ornaments, etc. Really beautiful wrought-iron decorations, incorporating

17

the second tank and/or assorted shelves at differing heights and sizes to hold books, flowers, concealed lights, and so on, are widely available — again at very reasonable cost. The bookcase stand is a standard sales item for example. If the legs of the stands are being made especially slim for better effect, it can help to splay them forwards or sideways for greater stability. Skirting boards can easily be accommodated by making a suitable kink in the leg, say 20cm (8in) up from the floor, and so saving space by not having the stand projecting out from the wall an unnecessary 5cm (2in).

To help the poor old dealer save storage space, knock-down versions are increasingly being marketed and are a real boon to the mail-order customer, as well as to carry-it-away yourself types. Ever tried to pack a 90cm × 30cm × 30cm (36in × 12in × 12in) stand into the back of a family car together with the Saturday shopping, the kids home from school, and the squashable groceries?

Tanks can be hung from the ceiling, be put on (as well as in) the wall with brackets; be housed on tall fluted wood columns, singly or in multiple columns, often in a trio of a tall central column flanked by two shorter and more slender ones, interlaced or not according to taste.

CHAPTER THREE

HEATING THE HOME
FIT FOR THE FISH

In these days of an affluent society, tropical fish ask for their share of central heating too; for some of us humans it's a welcome, or unobtainable luxury, but for the fish it is literally a matter of life or death. Most tropicals have a wide temperature tolerance but an ideal of 22°–26.5°C (72°–80°F) is best for long lived health. Of course, they can go down to 7°C (45°F) for relatively short periods of a few hours although they can drear on in lethargic misery at 20°C (68°F) for months or more, but that's just like taking a man from the equator and making him live in the arctic snows, unless he grumbled enough to make you do something about it. Similarly, at the other extreme fish wilt at 35°C (95°F) or more as the increased temperature automatically lowers the oxygen content of the water. Again, they can survive, especially with aeration, but tend to weaken.

However, these rules are not as hard and fast as they were once, mostly because of air travel. In the old days fish were bred locally, say in the same continent, but now they are regularly imported from hitherto quite inaccessible regions deep in forests, swamps, a thousand miles or more up river in shallow streams, dense in the jungle. The local temperatures are often 32°–43°C (90°–110°F) in the shade, and fish make the air journey to your dealer in one day! No wonder they need to be acclimatized. Chocolate Gourami are typical of such fish, coming from the swampy interior of Malaysia and thriving at 35°C (95°F) they deteriorate rapidly unless very carefully accustomed to lower temperatures. And they are such lovely fish, who have been given a bad name of being weak mostly because of cold.

Two golden rules for all and especially for those in Europe or America:

(1) For sustained temperatures of over 26.5°C (80°F) aeration and/or filters are particularly helpful, the higher the temperature the greater the water circulation required to offset the lowered oxygen content of the water and the subsequent increased danger of fouling.

(2) The whole tank has to be heated; particularly the very bottom where the catfish rest. If there are stratified layers or areas of hot and cold then the fish suffer as you and I would if continually forced to leave a warm room, go out into the cold, return, go out again, and so on. Hence the heater should be placed horizontally right down in the very very lowest area of the tank and heat right through from below up. Water circulation sufficient to diffuse the heat evenly should be maintained either by aeration or by fish, numerous and active enough to ensure this. This stratification of the water will explain many a mysterious 'going off their food' or 'growing listless', and particularly applies to some of the more exotically designed tanks that have 'out-lying areas' of water far from the heater, with weak water circulation.

Climatic conditions govern the strength of the heater required to maintain the optimum 22°–26.5°C (72°– 80°F) as does the local situation of the tank — draughts or abutting right up to a window (see page 16) can make heavy calls on the heater especially in the 2 am to 4 am period when the ambient temperature is as its lowest. But we give below the strengths for London and for southern England that experience has proved best.

45cm × 25cm × 25cm (18in × 10in × 10in) tank
                — 75 watts (100 in cold site)
45cm × 30cm × 30cm (18in × 12in × 12in) tank
                — 100 watts (125 in cold site)
60cm × 30cm × 30cm (24in × 12in × 12in) tank
                — 125 watts (150 in cold site)
90cm × 30cm × 30cm (36in × 12in × 12in) tank
                — 200 watts (250 in cold site)
120cm × 30cm × 30cm (48in × 12in × 12in) tank
                — 300 watts (375 in cold site)

In tanks of 90cm × 30cm × 30cm (36in × 12in × 12in) it is best to put two heaters of 100 or 125 watts each, rather than one of a bigger wattage; partly because of more even heat distribution, partly because of cost, and partly because of reliability and replacement ease. But the heater has to be right down in the very bottom two centimetres of the tank, as already stressed, and the tank decor discussed later in Chapter 8 will allow for this.

Making the heater unnecessarily strong merely throws an unfair burden on the thermostat which wears out quicker, sticks, and boils your fish. If you wish to be ultra-cautious then put the additional heater on a separate thermostat of its own. Experience at Fish Tanks Ltd of selling hundreds upon thousands of tanks over the decades has more than justified the reliability and long service of the above recommended strengths for rect-angular shaped tanks; speciality tanks with curving arms, sweeping areas, outlying limbs, etc., are in a class by themselves and need a specialist dealer to guide you.

Heaters are usually sold in varying strengths; a specialist dealer will keep them at 25w, 40w, 50w, 60w, 75w, 100w, 125w and 150w with a few stronger ones for special jobs. The good old type of a pyrex glass test-tube with the heating coil wound round an inner core, is still the unbeatable favourite, having lasted since pre-war days! It is quite a record.

One rather important point to watch and one that not every pet shop dealer will be able to satisfy is that the flex from the heater should be really long enough. Consider that the flex has to travel inconspicuously down the corner of the tank (right, but right to the very very bottom), along the bottom (buried out of sight) under the sand to the optimum spot from the point of decor (see Chapter 8) and of heat distribution, and you may come to rue the day your heater flex is too short and you have the darn thing hanging in full view with the vital bottom two centimetres of your tank cold, and your catfish ill.

Of course the pyrex test tube is being challenged by magnetic strip heaters, metal heaters, extra-long, extra-slim (and extra easy to break) heaters, by unbreakable plastic heaters (a strong contender), flexible rubber-covered wires to bury under the sand, etc. However, whatever your taste and your tank, there will certainly be a suitable heater readily available.

The thermostat to control the heater and to switch it on/off within a set range has also survived basically unaltered since pre-war days, and by now must have been sold literally in millions. It, too, is the good old pyrex glass test-tube housing a bi-metallic strip which bends unevenly with temperature change to make and break contact, and so to switch the heater on and off. Simple, functional, efficient.

Refinements galore have come, and most have gone. A neon light incorporated to show when the heater is on (or off) is a popular improvement. So, too, are heavier-duty ones to switch the aerator and even the tank's top lighting on and off with the heat. This applies mostly to tanks that are left unattended for long periods

while the family are on holiday, or for other particu-
larised uses like breeding. Many have been, and are, the
attempts to combine the heater with the thermostat, in
spite of the obvious disadvantages of housing the heater
directly with the thermostat, and of the rather bulky
unit so produced. Fully submersible thermostats still
out-sell those with external adjustments knobs (which
get accidentally knocked or twiddled with by well
meaning friends). The same applies to external thermostats that stick on to the outside of the tank glass —
protective caps and push-guards over the knobs notwithstanding.

Like the heaters, and the tanks, the choice is fabulous;
you would indeed be fussy not to find just what you
needed, easily and cheaply.

With thermometers, too, the choice is as great.
Legibility of the figures is important, especially as the
instrument is usually hidden out of sight, and so too is
their durability as some rub off or fade in use. Circular
stick-on thermometers are beginning to replace the more
usual glass tubular mercury or even spirit columns, as
their bi-metallic spring loading principle has been found
to be neat and reliable. A useful tip is to place at twelve-
o'clock-high the favourite temperature you want, say
25.5°C (78°F), so that the circular thermometer needle
is vertical; any deviation from the vertical will readily
indicate the temperature change without you having to
peer at the figures. Useful, too, is to place the thermometer half-way up the height of the tank: hot water
rises, so that a thermometer placed high up or low down
tends to give unnecessarily false readings, especially if
the water circulation is insufficient and temperature
stratification exists.

All parts of the heating unit, the heater, the thermostat and the thermometer, are functional rather than

decorative and should be housed strictly out of sight. There is no need to allow them to be seen or heard. Chapter 8 on decor gives tips on how the rocks, plants and ornaments can be arranged to achieve this. Little plastic (and other material) holders to clip the glass tubes into chosen areas and angles are helpful accessories, so too are multi-unit 'junction boxes' neatly to connect the leads from the various electrical necessities and to get rid of that mass of tangled wires. Your specialist dealer would do all this for you normally. Better ones have a service where they will come to your home to install the tank, or, at least, to do the wiring for you in the shop so that you have only to plug in when you get home.

If your tank is marine, or if you plan to convert it later, then do ensure that there are no metal parts on your heater clips or other accessories.

CHAPTER FOUR

AIR CONDITIONING
THE HOME FIT FOR
THE FISH

Aerators and Filters

In several very widely-sold earlier books air pumps have
been played down by me because, as they were then,
the pumps were noisy — or dear — and a tank 'balanced'
without aeration was normal. Aeration has now become
standard, although tanks can still be kept healthy even
in gruelling conditions without aerators/filters, because
two new factors caused a change during the 1970s:
a real technical break-through, and a rising standard of
living which makes the public more ready to buy what
were formerly optional extras. In America aeration has
been a 'must' for a long long time, but not in Europe —
until towards the end of the 1960-70 period.

The technical break-through has been two-fold: the
Americans with the magnetic coil, and the Germans
with the water cooled unit; both of which give a pump
that really is silent, really will run day and night without
over-heating, really has enough strength, and is not
unduly expensive. Other nations, including the English
and the Japanese have noted and have copied. Aerators
and filters are now clearly approaching the status of a
standard fitting. A third factor has been the marked
improvement in the old-established vibrator air pumps.
These have always been cheap, and became increasingly
noisy as the 'rubber bellows' inside them were worn
out and pumped vibration rather than air. Newer versions
with lateral bellows replacing the older vertical ones,

25

using better 'rubber' substitutes, are longer lasting and more and more powerful and have transformed the pumps radically. The claims of their makers as 'silent' and even as 'strong' have a meaning now that a sceptical public would have denied in earlier days. And they are still cheap.

So aeration has firmly come to stay, and the choice available is again fabulous. Refinements like bleed-off valves to ease back-pressure, like air-volume control knobs, like replacement 'bellows' for the vibrators, are all common, and the customer usually has umpteen makes and some five nationalities to pick from at prices ranging from schoolboy to millionaire; mostly schoolboy.

As a direct result several improvements have ensued:

(1) Perhaps most important of all, at long long last you can now keep a tank in a bright spot without getting pestered by that filthy slimy clinging clogging green algae! Remember the stuff! Who hasn't been plagued by it? Algae grows very fast under strong lights, including sunlight, and used to overrun the tank; it still grows in such conditions but the filters powered by the new pumps can easily cope with its rate of reproduction and maintain the tank clean and clear — a really big advance. Now you can house your beautiful, decorative, richly planted fish tank in your sun lounge, shop windows, big-windowed showroom, entrance hall or boardroom; an open air arcade, garden-walk; amid arc lights, spot lights or whatever.

But the old golden rules still apply, and your air pump and filter must be big enough for the job. You would not expect to power an aircraft carrier with the outboard motor of a dinghy, and the rule is still true that when a filter gets clogged up and saturated it tends to cease work and worse still to pump back foul poisoned

26

water. You need to clean it, and the frequency of the cleaning depends on the size of the filter and its ratio to the work. Sunlight, for instance, is usually measured in millions of candle-power, so beware of too small a filter.

(2) You can now keep more fish with a given air-surface of water than before; improved water circulation from filters, as distinct from air bubbles from a diffuser stone, give quicker absorption of oxygen into the water and faster elimination of noxious gases and particles. The golden rule for fish capacity of tropicals of average length of 3cm ($1\frac{1}{4}$in) was:

45cm × 30cm (18in × 12in) air surface — 18-20 fish
60cm × 30cm (24in × 12in) air surface — 24-28 fish
90cm × 30cm (36in × 12in) air surface — 36-40 fish
120cm × 30cm (48in × 12in) air surface — 48-54 fish

Old type aeration increased this by 40 per cent; the new power filters can lift the increase to up to 60 – 70 per cent; but you mustn't cheat – *power* filters are meant, not just aeration.

(3) With increased water circulation are eliminated problems of temperature differences in layers as stratification disappears, including the vital two centimetres at the bottom.

(4) From a design point of view greater freedom the shape of the tank means more original shapes and forms. The golden rule of air surface holds true, of course, but rapid circulation means ever-changing surface and greater absorption as the whole volume of flowing water is constantly brought into play.

(5) In natural life fish are often accustomed to running streams, with their eddies and surges; now these can all be reproduced in your fish tank by a luxurious

27

combination of a power filter, an under gravel filter and aeration. This triple unit really is luxury, but repays its cost in fish health and fascination. For example, why waste the power of the returning stream water? Let it fall from a centimetre above water and trap myriad dancing air bubbles to frolic through the water. Let it sweep across the air surface almost horizontally to clear off any top scum that would normally increase the surface tension of the water and so inhibit the oxygen absorption rate, not to mention fouling the fish food in its oily scum. Let it jet deep into the heart of the tank to flush out dusty corners, or to bounce off a chosen rock so as to wave and sway some graceful plants, or even to power the rotation of an ornamental wheel or windmill. There are so many lovely uses, and all help the health and joy of the fish, who will respond and play all the more. There are many fish like the zebra Danios that delight in fighting their way upstream and repeatedly will dive into the jet of water and play and surf ride, and helter-skelter downstream in gales of fish laughter.

Types of Filters

The good old box filter with a layer of activated carbon and white wool to trap the loose floating particles is still going strong and is still the most popular. Of course, there have been improvements. The activated charcoal is far more effective in absorbing hostile bacteria, noxious gases, fish urine (a very important factor, too often overlooked) than before; the horrible glass-wool that splintered in your hand has long since passed into the museum archives, and the latest plastic-based 'wools' have completely taken over.

In the design of the box filter itself two main developments have come to stay. The base of the box has been removed (or perforated) to allow suction up direct from the sand covering the tank bottom, and thus giving a far wider field of cleaning; limited only by the strength of the air pump causing the suction. Secondly, the air stream from the pump now often is diverted into an auxiliary chamber to give a most pleasing and beautiful effect of dancing air bubbles, as well as the normal cleaning suction.

Also entrenching itself is the under-gravel filter, in which the dirt is collected out of sight but is none the less ever-present, in the filter buried under the tank sand. Everything looks clean, but the dirt is still there; merely it has been 'swept under the carpet'. But the public insist on buying these under-gravel filters, which have responded by improved surface area, improved water circulation, and, hence of improved efficiency. Like them or not, they are obviously here to stay.

By far and away the most efficient filters are the containers external to the tank and powered by the water-cooled pumps especially, and by the magnetic-coiled circulating ones. By having the filter chamber quite separate and outside the tank you can get one truly big enough and really capable of heavy duty work. Many will last a whole year without cleaning and, incredible as it may seem, run constantly that whole time without over-heating or attention. It really is wonderful. One important point to watch though, especially for the water cooled ones — do not let the water syphon break. When started these pumps have to be 'primed' i.e. the pump container, the inlet tube and the outlet tube have all to be completely full of water, free of air bubbles, so that the water circulates freely; if this water circulation is broken, say by the inlet tube coming out of the tank water, then the pump rapidly empties itself (no new water coming into it from the inlet tube) and overheats through lack of water.

Other than that the filter is flawless.

Neat refinements continually come forth for many models like 'easy-pack' carbon replacements, disposable cartridges to save cleaning or washing out; granular chemicals mixed in with the glass wool so making the activated carbon unnecessary; neat cradles to hold the external filters so that they can be hung on to the tank sides or rear, if there is no shelf nearby. Filters should all be kept at tank water level and not housed above or below. This can be a bore, but it still is an essential precaution.

Ozoniser
The very latest in cleanliness technique is a sort of aquarist's space gun which emits O_3 instead of the conventional oxygen O_2 and whose extra-concentration kills bacteria. Because relatively small dosages can be lethal to fish it is usual to play the ozoniser on to the filter, from which the flow then goes to the tank. If no such buffer as the filter is possible then it may help to play the ozoniser O_3 stream on to a rock from which the stream bounces off, diffused rather than concentrated.

A most useful accessory, still somewhat rare and somewhat expensive, it is certain to grow more popular. By it the sterilisation of a tank can be done easily in minutes, rather than the old-fashioned clean and boil and scrub techniques. Periodic short doses are favoured by some, rather than a steady extra-low permanent stream.

Apart from the danger to the fish, this O_3 stream kills the helpful as well as the hostile bacteria, and its use obviously demands care. For marines, it is almost a 'must'.

CHAPTER FIVE

LIGHTING THE HOME
FIT FOR THE FISH

The simple things of older days still survive — one electric bulb of 25 watts per 30cm² (1ft²) of air surface and per 30cm (12in) of water depth held 5cm (2in) above water surface; for decades this has done great service, and so continues now. Usually the bulbs are housed in a metal cover fitting snugly all-over the tank top keeping in the fish, and keeping out dust, cats and small children; unobtrusive drip flanges feed back the condensation into the tank, so reducing evaporation especially if the air temperature of the room is colder than that of the tropical tank itself — a situation that encourages rapid water evaporation. Nice little air vents in the side of the metal cover just sufficient for ventilation, but not enough to accelerate evaporation, are also fitted. It was, and is, functional, efficient and cheap; it was, and is, popular.

Kept on for eight hours a day in a normal room this system grows the plants nicely without letting the green slimy algae become too obvious, and gives a pleasant all-over diffused light restful to the human eye. Darker rooms like basements could do with eight to ten hours per day, and brighter ones with sunlight present could be reduced right down to four hours, depending on how the plants thrived and the algae didn't. Too much light produces excess algae; the bulbs may be too strong, they may be lit for too long, or the room could be too bright, in which case the tank could be re-sited in a

31

darker spot, or be shaded from the natural daylight, e.g. by some books, a photograph, i.e. something large enough to throw sufficient shadow; or have a filter fitted as described in Chapter 4.

The bulbs are easy to replace (with one of the same strength of only 25 watts), but if they blow too often the cause is nearly always because the tank is not sitting level but is sloping backwards. Perhaps the floor or the table, etc., on which it sits is slightly sloped or uneven. Instead of dropping forward into the tank the water condensation then tends to seep backwards to the electric bulbs and blow them. A simple cure is to raise the metal cover fractionally at the rear, even 2mm ($\frac{1}{16}$ in) or jamming a matchstick between it and the tank top would do, so that the condensation flows forward again.

Some people like to have feeding holes cut into the all-over metal covers, to which we always fit sliding metal discs to keep the holes closed when not in actual use in order to inhibit water evaporation.

Other people prefer the cover to stop short some 10 to 15 cm (4 to 6in) from the front of the tank and to have a hinged flap for easier feeding and maintenance. This can be very useful unless the flap is too wide in proportion to the cover so that the light is on the rear part of the tank mostly, leaving the front in shadow. Should this happen you can fit auxiliary lighting to restore the plant growth, sometimes a spot-light, or all manner of helpful variations as will be described below.

For most people the covers are so light and pliable, usually made of rustless aluminium, that feeding holes and hinged flaps are superfluous.

Plastic is beginning to replace aluminium as the basic material for the cover. Stamped out in great numbers for standardized sizes these plastic covers are amazingly low in price. They have, too, the endearing quality of all plastics of 'letting light travel' through them to give a warm glowing-all-over effect that is definitely attractive.

Fluorescent tubes and striplights have never competed successfully with the more usual ordinary household light bulb, speciality uses of restricted space apart, but the 'Gro-lux' type of American lighting has begun a massive invasion since the end of the 1960s. In essence this 'Gro-lux' cuts out the 'yellowish' caste given by the household bulb and highlights the blues, reds, greens, etc., of the fish and plant colours; the light is 'gin clear', and certainly enhances most fish. Delicate hues that were often lost in the yellow caste are brought right out, and the public have understandably fallen for it in a big way. It is more expensive, and more complicated to fit, but it's well worth it. Wiring diagrams are usually supplied with the do-it-yourself kits and many people seem to cope quite happily. For the more-busy or the less-practical you can always call on the specialist dealer to do it for you.

Many indeed are the most beautiful variations that can be done, to please both the fish and the customer. In their natural habitats both are accustomed to changing lights, of varying intensities and angles: for the fish there is not only the change from dawn − noon − dusk, but every varying foliage and vegetation and changing water depths, all of which mean fluctuations and variety. For the customer there is the bright glare of the cocktail party or the hushed peace of the headache, so both like alternative lighting in the fish tank. At dusk, or in other subdued light, it is extraordinarily soothing and relaxing to sit with only the light of the fish tank, calmly radiating; then as the dusk deepens to night, try switching off the (relatively bright) top lighting of the tank and put on the even softer diffused auxiliary rear-lighting that gently glows through the whole width of the placid waters of your tank. Tensions ease out, insomnia and worries just melt, replaced by a gentle yet living silence. Often the rear of the tank is painted in a lovely soft colour, thickened here and there, to silhouette a 'line of distant mountains', and the real light shining back to you through this 'view', fronted by the waters of your fish tank, just joyous and effective only in soft light and in gentle moods.

Another version is to have secondary lighting concealed in the tank stand, especially if this is a decorative one housing plants, ornaments, and so on. Gayer and very stimulating tank versions have an automatic on/off sequence usually in a run of three: 'on' a bright white light, 'off' a subdued light, and then back to the original white light to re-start the sequence. The pauses between changes are quite dramatic, as is the total presentation. A further very pleasant variation on this triple sequence is to have two with diffused light (say a coloured and a white) and the third with an intensely focused light which sends a single narrow shaft to one chosen spot only in the tank. At this spot we put a strong motif, a reflective metal, a moving part like a wheel or a dancing air stream, a waving plant, a floating strip of featured plastic — all manner of delightful touches, so easy for you to express yourself and your mood. And, of course, the fish love it too.

Naturally, there are fundamental rules imposed by Mother Nature which a wise man obeys. The nearer you sit to the tank, the more focused can be your light; at the far end of the room soft diffusion is more harmonious. Again, too intense a focus for too long will invite algae, so direct the light beam on to a substance that is inhibiting to algae, such as metals, resins and crystals. The ratio of overall light to the room should not be too great, or the pleasant focus turns into a glaring hypnotic distraction. And, above all, the balance of the tank must be maintained — the plants and the fish must be happy too; as indeed they are intermingled with areas of shade and light, of brilliant shafts and streaky glens or crevices, so that they too can choose according to their mood of the moment.

CHAPTER SIX

FURNISHING THE
HOME FIT FOR
THE FISH

Artistry, love and understanding for the fish, skill in execution of design, practical rules ensuring long service, these are among the truths that soon begin to differentiate between the pet shop man and the specialist dealer. A sensitive awareness is more important than crude flash, and the next three chapters seek to illustrate this, to help to achieve it.

Having got a big enough tank, with a big enough air surface (or power filter), nicely positioned, warmed and lit, you can now set about making the interior look gorgeous, creating the aquascape in fact.

Let us start with the sand at the base of the tank. It needs to be fine enough for the fish to pick up in their mouths, to swill round, to forage into, to dig into, to rub against, to hollow out, to lay eggs in, to pick up and to blow against rocks so cleaning their surface and preparing them for adhesive eggs; in short, it has to be fine enough! But not so fine that it will matt down preventing all this happy activity, choking the plants as their roots are restricted from spreading easily. Nor must it be too coarse, again preventing the above everyday activities and entrapping particles of food that lie and rot between its wide crevices. It has to be just right, and should be a lovely golden colour. No wonder it is sometimes brought all the way from the Channel Islands and sold by the ton.

Love of colour, and fear of oil pollution has activated

the sale of 'artificial sands' made of an ever-widening circle of materials, starting with crushed stones, crushed coral, and believe it or not dyed cork which finally sinks when saturated and 'treated'. Yellow, white, black, green, red, and blue, mixed or pure; in streaks, in patterns, in squares; dividing the tank floor laterally, horizontally; accentuating this, focusing away from/to/ by/in that; all sorts of gay fun is yours for the enterprise. But Mother Nature still rules: the darker the tank floor (at least in suitable patches) the better the colours of the fish and the more restful to the catfish, and the consistency must be of the Channel Island natural sand described above. Finally, it must be, positively, non-toxic to fish, all dyes being fast, for example.

Not everyone seems to realise that rocks dissolve appreciably in water, altering what is technically known as 'the total dissolved solids' and so harming the fish. Many a gradual listless decline and death has its origin here quite unsuspected. That weather beaten, full of holes and worn shapes, Westmorland rock is very nice to behold, but is a pernicious death-trap since it dissolves far too readily. The 'hard' stones, free of lime, awkward to mine, difficult to break into attractive pieces are the ones Mother Nature insists we use: these may come all the way from the far south-west, such as the black Devon rock, streaked with grey. These grey streaks are 'hard' and, therefore, harmless as contrasted to the more readily available quartz or crystalline veins that look good, but dissolve quickly. You want to be careful about all this.

Rock substitutes have not been slow to come forward. For decades, now, we have been using the beautiful, just beautiful, coloured crystal lumps — streaked and veined, translucent, opaque, strong colours, delicate see-through pastels, even pure white or pitch black;

37

easily wiped clean, impossible for algae to 'pit-into', one wipe and the horrible green stuff comes off.

Plastics, too, have played their part, as you would expect. Our 'martian' rock in gnarled, entwined, heavy threaded balls, or jutting two-tone super impositions, has long been popular. So too have artificially made plastic or fibre glass 'rocks' stamped out (hollow) in many shapes and sizes, or even as 'walls', 'stone balustrades', 'steps', 'arches', and an ever changing list of decorative items.

Fluorescent-type plastics that glow in the dark, or gleam in light are ever becoming more prominent, for rocks, for ornaments and for sand.

Your choice is great.

There is no reason, too, why you should not use 'unconventional' things like Venetian glass vases; holes can be drilled in the base (sacrilege, say some) to allow a limited amount of water circulation and then used as decorative flower pots. Or vases can be mounted on tall stems or columns so as to catch the light, sway in an air stream, or be positioned just in the right spot at the correct angle, which need not be vertical.

Family, or other personal motifs can be rendered non-toxic and used; as can glass, silver or even gold bangles and bracelets; futuristic strips, loops and cut-outs of chosen coloured plastics, old weathered twigs, 'logs', nicely shaped sprays cut from a tree. Have you any idea how attractive tree bark looks in strips or chunks or half-moon? If the tank is big enough why not also incorporate under-water lights inside? Waterproofing is not difficult. It is amazing what you can do with plain old bamboo sticks, cut to size and suitably arranged.

Again the choice is fabulous, and is yours. But make sure that everything is non-toxic: the glue to join bits, the screws, the lengths of wire, the elastic, the clips, springs, nuts and bolts — everything! There are all manner of ways for treating these things to render them non-toxic.

CHAPTER SEVEN

ARRANGING THE FURNISHINGS
FOR THE HOME FIT FOR
THE FISH

Having thus an almost endless choice of furnishings, which are you going to buy, and how are you going to arrange them? Unless, of course, you send for a reputable specialist, such as Fish Tanks Ltd, who are willing to design tanks at home and abroad.

Your own taste, your room, and the distance away you plan to sit would have to be considered. If your tank will be alongside your chair, then detailed minuteness and finesse in colour/patterns could be appreciated, muted or gay according to taste; if sited more than a couple of metres away then broader sweeps would increasingly tend to predominate with greater distances, the all-over glance rather so that the tank frame, its interior aquascape and the surrounding room would have a joint priority, and be taken as a whole. These are degrees of emphasis; seldom are the rules of decor rigidly hard and fast. Of course, the whole tank must always blend with you and yours.

Begin with all the functional gadgets that simply have to be included, the heaters, thermostats, filters, lights and so on. These have all got to be kept definitely right out of sight. There must be no wires, tubes or whatever to be visible unless they are beautiful. You should even go round and peer at the thermometer. Beauty can and will predominate, and you buy these functional essentials in combinations and sizes to fit neatly away in the far corners and reaches of your layout.

Next, the sand. About 4cm $(1\frac{1}{2}in)$ would do just the plain job of providing a base for the plants to grow in but you will need far more in order to create banks and terraces. In a rectangular 60cm × 30cm × 30cm (24in × 12in × 12in) we put nearly 22kg (50lb) weight of sand. This sounds fantastic when a quarter of that will give more than 2.5cm (1in) of even depth.

In Chapter 8 are described the necessary but mundane details of how you wash the sand, the tools you need, and the technique of arrangement. Here, we are concerned with the artistic creative side for the moment.

Next we usually choose the rocks. These can be the very restrained natural ones only, or as is more usual mixed with the beautiful coloured crystals, for example, to be muted or gay according to taste again. The rocks do multiple work. Buried deep into the slope of piled up sand, they will hold the bank in place. The whole rock can be buried so that only one (very carefully chosen) side is visible and the rest is maintaining a firm grip to prevent the sand slope collapsing. Of course, the rocks are seldom used singly, but in lines, tiers, 'V' formations, arrowheads; squat heavy ones forming a support for one or more of varying shapes: tapering fingers to reach to the ceiling (and hide the thermostat tube, say), arches, caves, terrace walls, steps winding upwards straight or zig-zag. Extraordinarily arresting is colour mixed with natural to lead up to a highlight in the distance, to have a gentle sweep abruptly terminating in one strong coloured piece, to have a circle with a colour sprinkle within, to line the winding steps with coloured walls, to have a deep cave with something strong just discernible in the gloom, to have crevices in which Angel fish can lurk, to have overhanging ledges on to which the sucking catfish can cling, to have tiny gaps and hollows into which can crawl the spiny eels.

The joys are endless. But firmly hidden away have been the functional heaters, etc., and firmly anchored to prevent collapse have been all sand slopes, banks and so forth. The aquascape must not only look right now, but stay so; loose gaps soon allow sand to dribble away to a flat drear waste-land. That is why you will need plenty of large rocks, buried deep, not just small pieces dumped hopefully on to the sand. They must grip, really grip, and hold their station. For the same rectangular 60cm × 30cm × 30cm (24in × 12in × 12in) tank it is best to put in rocks of a total of some 22kg (50lb) weight. Again this sounds fantastic, again the key is that much is buried and is, therefore, functional, or is piled one on top of another, and, therefore, needs a large stable base.

Fish love, and need, little homes of their own and soon move into the crevices (flat thin fish like Angels, Scats, Discus, Gourami, etc.), into caves (Elephant Nose fish, who are tremendous stay-at-homes), ledges, nooks and crannies. Nothing is wasted, and much is the misery of those left out if there is not enough to go round. Simultaneously there should be free open spaces where the fast, the strong, the gregarious and the gossips can throng and swirl; where fights and courtships jostle with the throbbing pulse of ever moving life. Spare too a corner, sheltered, calm and not too brightly lit, for the weak and the indisposed; where the introvert and the shy can come into their modest own. After all, you are building a home fit for the fish, and they vary in character and temperament just as much as you and I can do.

Differing depths of water are a great boon, not all fish are strong divers and swimmers — the fat and the lazy are not unknown there either, nor too are the constitutionally constructed slow movers, not to mention the floor grubbers. In their natural habitat fish tend to stay in definite layers of the water: an upturned mouth (super terminal) means a surface swimmer; a forward pointing mouth (terminal) means that mid-waters are preferred; and a downward turned mouth (sub-terminal) means that vital area of water right down at the very bottom of the tank must also be kept warm and clean for these. So the aquascape that provides varying depths, as well as shelters and open space, is greatly appreciated by the fish and by the humans who like the look of a beautiful arrangement. Everyone is happy! The area of air-surface governs the rate of oxygen intake into the water, not the total volume.

Plants are an essential both for the decor and for the health balance of the tank which will be discussed in Chapter 8. Plants that are delicately green and ferny, swaying near a heavy fat anchor-rock softening its hard lines; tall reed-like plants in thick jungle-clumps in which lurk the quaint-shaped Hatchet fish; neat stubby little bushes half-hiding the entrance to an arch or a cave; great big heavy leafed ones to shelter tired eyes from the light, to support the clinging sucking catfish, to lay eggs on, to have a snooze tucked up inside the curl of these fine leaves. Waving palms, spiky grass, strong tall and almost frightening, delicate dancing spheres, light greens, dark greens, red tinged, thick stems, thin stems, see-through lace work or dense thick foliage, stubby and tall — you have a choice to please the most fastidious.

CHAPTER EIGHT

HELPFUL HINTS ON
SETTING UP THE TANK

Having got a broad picture of how you plan to furnish the home fit for the fish, we now come to the actual physical work of doing it, and the following order of sequence may help.

The interior of the tank wiped and cleaned, it is placed in position, and the 'exterior' work is tackled first. Is there a background to be stuck on to the outside of the tank at the back? Is there padding and protective hardboard, etc., to be placed between it and the window? Has enough room been left to get at the electric plugs, to fit an external filter, to house the bits of the toplight that may protrude so that it does not foul when lifted? Is the tank level, fully supported all round, in the position you want it to remain, central for example, backing up against an ornament or a picture on the wall?

Now, let us do the electric wiring while the tank is empty and dry; the toplight, which will need to be ready to switch on when we're doing the aquascape later, so that we can see exactly where the shafts of light fall; the thermostat, but make sure the heaters do not come on before the tank has been filled; the filters, especially the under-gravel ones; all the separate torpedo-switches for individually controlling the lighting, the aeration, etc., all finished, neat and tidy.

Next, the sand and rocks could be washed, this should not be done in the tank. A little sand at a time, rinsed and swirled and rinsed again and again until thoroughly, but thoroughly, clean and then put straight into the tank as each portion has been cleaned, rather than be left to dribble all over the place. What did you wash the sand in? If the bucket had soap, detergent or grease in it, then all that will have gone into your 'cleaned' sand and cause trouble.

The cleaned rocks and ornaments can be laid out on clean (thick absorbent) newspaper on the floor, so that you can see them at a glance and the more easily choose the right piece when you come to dress the tank.

You may have tubular glass heaters that need to be placed horizontally flat right down in the very bottom two centimetres of the tank. Yet the sand is being banked up several centimetres high, especially at the back where the heaters usually go — right out of sight. Rather like Moses holding back the waters of the Red Sea to allow his passage through, you put the heaters flat on the floor (with perhaps 1cm ($\frac{1}{2}$in) covering of sand to prevent them actually heating, and cracking the tank base) and hold back the sand by building a rock wall on either side, using big squat base rocks, on which can grip the ascending ones. Over these two retaining walls you could put a crosspiece of rock or tree bark to form an arch, a longish decorative rock (or rocks) horizontally on the floor in front of the heaters and these are securely hidden and protected. Make sure the heaters do not touch the tank rear glass, or that might crack too, and for beauty's sake please thread all heater wires neatly down the tank corners, buried under the sand, until they protrude just enough to allow the glass tubes to lie flat on the sand at the chosen spot. As you probably realise the glass parts of the heaters should not be buried but they certainly can be hidden behind or even (careful!) beneath a rock.

The glass thermostat can easily hang in the corner

down which you had threaded the heater wire, so hiding
both from view with one tall rock, and clump of plants,
or stream of air bubbles.

The filters and aerators will also have been strategically
placed out of sight, but functionally well sited. For
example, if there is an inlet tube of a power filter sucking
water out to be cleaned, then the end of the tube
obviously should be low down right over the sand, or
even in a hollow — carbon dioxide gas is breathed out
by the fish and is a heavy gas tending to settle on the
floor — and there should be no great impediments in the
flow of the water (and dirt) across to it. Of course, the
outlet tube returning the cleaned water will be in quite
another part of the tank, probably placed high up.

Having hidden your heaters, say under the arch made
of two retaining walls, as described, we suggest that you
build your aquascape as a whole, rather than concentrate on one end of the tank at a time. Basically, the
sand and rocks at the rear are piled high, you can even
break water surface if you like; anchored as you go by
burying deep, providing the nooks and crannies discussed
in the previous chapter; and gradually tending to slope
down to zero level in the front. Food dropped here then
has little sand to foul.

We slope the decor not only front to back, but left
to right, as well. There are no rigid rules: if good water
circulation is ensured the arch for the heaters need not
be central; the shallow sand where the food is given
need not be in the front, although fish tend to congre-
gate in the main feeding area; incidentally, you might
provide a subsidiary one for the weaker fish.

All the time you are doing this dressing you will be
remembering, or checking, how the light from your top-
light will strike. Into the areas of shade you will naturally
plant cryptocorines, for example, which can manage

46

well without too much light. Your best rocks, plants and motifs will go in the best spots, deliberately featured, with nothing detracting from them immediately near.

When the sand, equipment, and rocks have been finally arranged fill the tank only partially for easier planting. The fall of the incoming water can be broken by holding a plate at sand level, or by spreading a clean sheet of paper over it, so preventing the sand being churned up and clouding the water (especially if it had not been sufficiently well washed in the first place) until the tank is about half or three-quarters full.

Plants are best grouped, single items often look thin and sparse. Opinions vary as to whether to put different kinds of plant in any one group, some people insist that this close mixing inhibits growth, but many happy combinations have survived. Most plants grow tall, too much so for the average tank, and trail their leaves along the water surface; in moderation, one or two like this can be excellent. Nearly all plants can be pruned short without disfigurement. Some like light, others not so much. As a rough guide, the thicker the stem, the more likely is the plant to protrude right out of the water. Planting sticks are a little fiddly to use at this stage but are excellent for the final touches, reaching down to straighten a tangled stem, to open or close a bunch, to lean them in a particular direction the better to harmonise, screen or sway.

Grease, oil and detergents must be totally absent from the tools and buckets you use, whether to top up, wash plants in before use, or to keep fish in. Nor, too, is it prudent to keep these things near strong smelling paints, disinfectants, soaps and so on, particularly does this apply to cloths used to wipe the tank.

When all is finished the fish tank should look gorgeous, and be balanced.

Balance is vital for fish health. Through the large air-surface oxygen is absorbed into the water, helped by the aeration and/or power filters. Varying water depths are largely irrelevant, as it is the air surface, or water circulation, that counts. This fresh oxygen is taken in by the fish who breathe it out as carbon dioxide, a harmful gas that must be eliminated. Under the action of the toplight the oxygenating plants break down the carbon dioxide into carbon and oxygen, the carbon staying to fertilise the plants themselves and the oxygen going back to the fish. This process of photosynthesis keeps the water fresh and the tank balanced. Of course, the description here given is extremely simplified and does little justice to the whole new science of water composition, content and condition but will serve as a guide.

Any one factor will affect the whole, but you particularly need to watch: (a) excess food, fouling at the bottom and encouraging hostile bacteria, (b) excess light causing algae, (c) too many, or too big, fish consuming oxygen faster than the air-surface takes it in from the air, (d) insufficient (and more rarely, excess) plants.

When in doubt, ask your specialist dealer.

CHAPTER NINE

SERVICING THE TANK

Where else can you get a pet that needs so little care? That does not have to be taken out for exercise or it will mess on the carpet. That can be left without food for a fortnight while you are on holiday. That will not make a noise or annoy the neighbours while you're out. That takes up so little room, that lights up that part of the room into a lovely focal point, that has such beautiful colours, such intriguing shapes, such fascinating antics, that gives birth direct to live baby fish, that comes when you call, that is silent, that costs so little and gives so much.

Servicing takes only a few minutes per day, far far less than you and I demand!

Daily servicing
Scarcely much more than putting on the top-light and feeding.

If there is no filter then there is a tendency in modern cities for an oily scum to settle on the tank water surface; like a housewife skimming fat off soup you can remove this by laying a piece of newspaper flat all over the water surface, and gently drawing it off horizontally, not lifting it off vertically. As the paper is dragged off low and flat, the scum is removed. Obstinate little pockets in inaccessible places like the thermostat corner, can be gently paddled out into the open with your finger, and then cleared off with paper, horizontally low and flat.

A very much more thorough way, necessary only in cases of exceptionally heavy scum, is to immerse a clean (no smell of pickles or tobacco!) jar tail downwards vertically into the tank. When the lip of the jar just, only just, sinks below water surface the top layer (of scum water) rushes into the jar which should be lifted gently just before it fills. Repeated operations will soon remove the top centimetre of water, and all the scum.

A refinement of the above is to use a piece of paper lying flat on the surface and steered to concentrate the scum in one area into which the jar is then lowered, tail first, to suck in much scum with relatively little water.

During all these operations, the aerator is best switched off, allowing a few moments for churned up scum to rise to the surface for easier removal.

The careful aquarist will see at a glance that the water temperature is right, that the fish are not listless or having drooping fins, that there are no signs of cloudy water or of fouling, e.g. sand going black where too much food has been dropped and decayed. All the work of short duration, literally of just a few minutes.

Weekly servicing
Using one of many available types of syphons or of underwater cleaners, the excess mulm, decaying leaves and other debris should be removed. The tank glass inside be wiped with a 'scraper' bought for the purpose, or with a clean (must be clean) small cloth and the tank topped up with new water of the same temperature as the tank (using a clean, but clean, jug or bucket). It is a good idea also to wipe the sides and back of the tank glass, going 'upstream' so as not to flatten any slopes of banked-up sand.

A quick skim to remove the top scum, some food,

and the whole job need have taken far less time than a man needs to shave.

Monthly servicing

Basically, the same as for the weekly, except that the rocks, plants and filters may want attention whether you do it, or send for us. Time required? Rather like a thorough hair wash plus bath plus pedicure.

Plants grow stalky at the bottom as they grow tall. They can be uprooted, their stems shortened down to where the foliage starts, and be replanted. New roots will soon grow.

Vallisneria, and other varieties that send out reproductive shoots, cannot be so shortened but their tall leaves and stems can be pruned from the top, or even be thinned out by hiving off parts from the main core.

The rocks can be wiped gently and slowly in situ; or be turned round to expose a new face and to bury the former one so as to allow any algae to die naturally; or be removed to be scrubbed clean (no soap, detergent or grease on the scrubbing brush). The removal and replacement is best done one rock at a time, so as not to disturb the aquascape too much.

The beautiful coloured crystals do not allow the algae to grip, and a simple wipe is usually sufficient.

The filter carbon and wool may have to be changed. It all depends on the type. A good guide is the colour of the originally white wool; if too dark, then why not a clean and change of both? In olden days people often forgot the quite serious effect of fish urine and used to change only the wool assuming that this got most of the muck, since it was the first contact with the incoming dirty water and had to trap all the floating debris, etc. Yet the invisible urine also choked the activated-carbon quicker than was often realised, so that a change of both is advised.

The filter will clean only till it is saturated. Then it pours back water as dirty, or worse, than it receives. A sobering thought, especially if the climate of the day is hot and sultry.

A syphon up, not removing too much of the water, a wipe (uphill) of the glass, a top up with water of the same temperature, a skim, and a feed.

Imagine the work on food alone that it's taken to keep you and me going for a month!

A clean-right-out and re-set of the aquascape
Quite a job, with lots of bits and pieces, rather like redecorating the kitchen, and done as infrequently. Naturally, the professional will do it more quickly, in fact you might even feel slightly annoyed at the way he clips hours off the time you would have taken.

Get all the essentials ready first, so as least to disturb the fish, and so as to be able to complete the job without having to stop for meals.

Buy new sand, and wash, wash, wash and re-wash it till it is truly clean — that is a good hour gone. Have ready at least two clean, really clean, buckets, one for topping up, the second to house the fish while you re-do the tank. Also have ready other, not necessarily clean, buckets into which you can syphon out the dirty water. If the tank water is clean, though the sand is not, then additional (clean) buckets would be needed to save this clean old water for the final topping up operation.

Have ready plenty of cloths, newspapers for the floor protection. Where are you going to place on the floor the rocks, spread out in the order of removal for easier replacement. What are you going to wash them in?

Have you got two nets for catching the fish? The larger one to hold in position ready to be pulled up-wards, not forwards, when the fish has been driven into it by the second and smaller net. Your syphon tubes? Spare carbon and wool? Any heating unit that needs replacement? New plants?

Now have your 'tea-break' so that you are ready to do a start-to-finish-job. Oh yes, have you got something to cover the bucket that will house the fish, so as to prevent them jumping out?

Start by making a mental note of the fish that will be difficult to catch, and count their number, so that one is not forgotten. Eels, catfish, loach, small babies or neons, and other elusive ones.

Without disturbing the tank, switch off the aeration and/or filter, and the heater, though not the light, and syphon off to save in clean buckets as much of the old water as is worth re-using; perhaps half the tank.

Next remove the plants, gently rinse them in warm only water, lay them with their roots all to one end, cleaned and pruned ready for use. Keep damp.

Remove the rocks, scrub clean, and leave on floor in order for replacement.

If the filters are removable, you could do so now, and clean. If they are of the external type, outside the tank, you would probably have done so earlier.

Syphon off excess (and by now filthy) water till there are only 5—8cm (2—3in) left. Please take great care that you do not syphon out a fish by mistake; it is very easy to do, and you may have been prudent enough to have already bought a 'fish-tail' for your syphon tube, i.e. a gadget to prevent this tragedy.

With all the plants and rocks removed, and the water down to 8cm (3in), it should not be too difficult to catch the fish, housing them in some of the clean tank water first syphoned off. You may care to plug in the heating unit into this bucket before covering to prevent a frightened or an excited fish from jumping out.

Unless the tank interior has previously been sealed with the newer adhesives that bond glass to glass, never, but never, move the tank to get rid of the messy last 8cm (3in) of water. Water pressure will have normally maintained the glass bedded against the metal frame. Now that this pressure has been removed there is a distinct tendency for the glass to 'spring back' so causing a leak; moving the tank would make the tendency worse.

Instead, the water should be syphoned, the sand scooped out, the filters removed, and the tank rinsed, emptied and re-rinsed all without moving it; or without putting any pressure on the outside of the glass, e.g. by trying to wipe it clean at this stage. The inside can be wiped of course.

As soon as the interior has been cleaned, these gravel filters should be rinsed and replaced, the already-washed new sand put in, the heating unit fitted back neatly, and the cleaned rocks anchored back. All as quickly as possible, to minimise leaks.

Add new water to a depth of 5cm (2in), some 5°C (10°F) warmer than normal to reheat the sand and rocks (pouring on to a clean sheet of paper spread over the sand), then all feasible amounts of the originally saved matured water, more new water warm enough to bring the whole temperature up to the usual 22°–28°C (72°–82°F), leaving enough room for what you plan to re-use of the water now housing the fish.

Replace plants, then the fish and top up; now the outside glass can be cleaned.

Any final touches can be done at more leisure; skim the surface, and feed the fish; then at long last, you can feed yourself and rest and admire your handiwork.

It may happen that the whole disturbance has been too much for a particularly old or particularly nervous fish. If you suspect this possibility a kindly thought would be to have a separate container for such of our weaker brethren, in which they can be housed during the cleaning. You might even make a special effort to catch them first, and to replace them in the cleaned tank, also first. For a few days afterwards you could be extra surveillant lest the fish showed signs of strain. Live foods would be appreciated.

CHAPTER TEN

FEEDING

The main rule has been that all the food given to the fish is eaten in two or three minutes so that no excess drops to the bottom to foul the sand. This still holds good, but progress has come to this field too.

The old crumbled bread and biscuit mixture laughingly passed off as food was soon replaced by flakes — made to scientific formulae to hold a nutritious mixture, and designed to float on the water surface long enough for all the fish to feed. There are all manner of these flakes, various colours, various ingredients; some emphasising proteins, others vitamins, carbohydrates, etc; in large sizes for hand feeding big fish; even dyed to tinge the water to show that too many had been put in.

As change in diet is necessary for fish too, often the flakes are packed in 'menu' form, one type per day, ringing the changes over a sequence of four or seven.

A similar transformation had taken place in foods for baby fish; improving on the crumbs merely ground into finer particles came the liquidised foods, rather like tooth-paste squeezed a little at a time out of a tube. Excellent for the babies, but, as with their human counterparts, they tend to be messy. Nurseries seldom are the tidiest place in the home. The tricky stage is when the paste foods are outgrown and solid foods are attempted. As yet there is no substitute for the finer ground particle of flake or the even more chopped up live worm. Fortunately, this transitional period is short and nearly all survive to tackle the standard sizes. It may not be long before some enterprising manufacturer enters into this 'teenage' market too!

Next came the freeze-dried revolution, as it did for humans. Processed while fresh, and then frozen, keeping its fresh quality for long periods, these come in cubes to stick on to the tank glass allowing the fish to nibble for an hour even, as the cube slowly dissolves. The ingredients cover ever wider ranges — frozen tubifex worms, mosquito larvae, ants eggs, liver, shrimp, varied formulae designed for stimulating growth, or colour, or breeding.

Now the jelly-lumps are beginning to make their mark. Put a small plastic lump in a container and leave it there permanently, so that the fish can eat when they like, for as long as they like! It really is more 'natural' as fish have very short digestive tracts and need to nibble fairly constantly for ideal health. Their stomachs or yolk sacs are ill-adapted for storing food for long periods. Mother Nature intended them constantly to be searching for foods, and, at long long last, this 'jelly type' makes it possible in the fish tank. Over-feeding, or feeding little and often are both becoming obsolete.

Vacation blocks have long been known: a sort of layer upon layer of food done in a dome-shaped blob which dissolved slowly over fourteen days allowing out one small layer of food per day.

Automatic electric feeders, like time clocks, have (usually) fifteen notches to allow one per day of food for fifteen days, or three feeds per day for five days. The amount and type of food put in the fifteen 'containers' controlled by these notches being left to individual taste and choice. Excellent but expensive, their growth has been inhibited by the simple little vacation block and the permanent jelly-type foods, but they still survive.

So, too, do the truly live foods, living daphnia and live tubifex worms, for example, simply because the fish love them so, and have been known to stage hunger strikes if deprived of them for too long. In the old days it had to be collected early each morning and the customer had to call each day to pick it up. Now a weekly visit will suffice because the live daphnia can be packed in plastic bags pre-sealed with water, oxygen and food for the daphnia themselves so that the unit stays fresh and alive for a whole week. You simply buy seven bags, one per day, during your weekly visit.

Of course, all manner of containers are marketed to house the food in your tank: feeding rings for the floating flakes, some with trays below to catch the excess; perforated cones or trays to allow tubifex worms to wriggle through to the tank in small numbers; gadgets for circulating the water past live tubifex works so as to keep them fresh for days; containers holding live cultures of white worms, micro worms, grindal worms; and many, many others.

You should have no difficulty in giving the fish a balanced varied diet. Please don't forget the vegetarians of whom there are very many among the fish, and they resent lumps of meat being thrown at them. Four or seven different tins of food, of different types and/or makes, given in sequence over the days is good. It becomes ideal, if also varied with live daphnia for instance some four times a week.

The amount to give? Sufficient for a quick meal — long drawn out banquets are unknown among fish unless the jelly-type foods start the habit. How frequently do you give? Once, or perhaps twice a day, unless you are breeding or conditioning up special specimens in which case five feeds per day are not unknown. How do you give? In various places and at various depths, simultaneously, so that the weak and slow get some too in a sheltered back-water, so that the base inhabitants like the catfish are not left out when all the food floats.

What will the fish eat? Basically anything that you and I will; no more than us do they like greasy mess, or stale stinking foods, or floating flakes trapped in an oily scum at the water surface that should have been skimmed off first (Chapter 9). Like us, they too are adaptable. For example, if you really can't get live foods you could hang a small piece of meat, fish, shrimp, liver, prawn, roe; almost anything that does not dissolve too soon in water; cooked or raw, but washed to remove grease or blood; and hung in the tank on a bit of cotton for half an hour or so, allowing the fish to nibble. You could hang in more than one lump, at more than one depth, of more than one type. It is not too difficult to attach three lumps to one thread (bottom, middle and top), and your fish would certainly appreciate the kindness.

CHAPTER ELEVEN

PLANT CARE

Beautiful things, necessary for the balance of the tank
Two main kinds are available. Those that grow wild in
indigenous ponds and streams of Europe and America,
which tend to be a little too coarse and too big for the
indoor aquarium, and which can be sold (in summer)
very cheaply, often in bunches. Come winter, and these
plants tend to wither and die, and the steadier advantages
of buying the proper aquarium types become apparent.
This latter type are hothouse grown (an expensive process), are finer in texture, more suited in size and are
ideal for a tank. Not everyone seems to be able to distin-
guish between these two quite separate groups, until
they learn the hard way.

One of the troubles with the proper aquarium group
was that they too, of course, grew best in summer and
were then most plentiful. Yet demand for them reaches
its peak in winter and its trough during the warmer
months when the fish tank owner tends to go out of
doors and tends to neglect his tank and his television.
The problem has now been partially solved by flying
over imports from Asia during the winter months.
There is just one snag the discerning customer will
notice. Because of 'eye-appeal', and because some people
like to 'get a lot for their money', the tendency is to
import bigger individual specimens of plants than is
wise. An older plant is less adaptable than a younger
one, and is far more likely to shed its leaves and to cut

back its growth even to apparently dying (although patience will nearly always be rewarded by a new shoot). If you will consider the hot humid moist steamy air and rich river soils of Malaysia and then the sudden one-day air flight transfer to your tank, the advisability of a younger smaller plant becomes obvious; in the end it will grow bigger, quicker.

Fig. 1
Cryptocorine johorensis
Engler

Fig. 2
Cryptocorine longicauda
(Becc.)

Fig. 3
Cryptocorine griffithii

Fig. 4
Cryptocorine lingua (Becc.)

Some Popular Plants

61

This question of rich soil has to be seen in perspective. If only the plants were to be considered then such soil would have to be provided, yet this would also encourage the growth of hostile bacteria, algae, and other things that would swing the tank balance too far away from optimum fish health. However, the dilemma has been solved in practice: at the moment of transfer of new plants, when their need for a boost is greatest, you can use one of the many chemicals specially sold to do just this job. These come either as pellets for insertion at the plant base at the time of transplanting, or more usually as liquids to be added to the tank water. Both have a limited-time action allowing the tank balance gradually to go back to normal, as the plant boost fades and the new roots thrive. You may too, increase the duration of the top-lighting by 10 per cent or so, during this sensitive period of seven to twenty-one days; of course, these are rough guides only, so much depending on local conditions. Lowering the tank temperature 1°C (2°F) can also help during this same period, particularly in the autumn when plants naturally tend to 'rest' as the sap tends to withdraw rather than rise. If, however, your new plant came from Malaysia or from the Amazon, as it probably did, with a local temperature of 27°–35°C (80°–95°F) then a slight temperature increase would be preferable.

These suggestions are applicable mostly to the more rare and delicate varieties; many you can just simply bung in.

Certain types and sizes of fish love to uproot any plant; you could then protect it by planting in a small (decorative?) flower pot suitably holed to allow the roots to expand out into the tank base.

Plants will tell you their troubles if you will only listen: leaves that go pale, plant roots are too cramped, or too hot; light too strong, or too weak; temperature too high or low; merely the normal seasonal time of rest; fish mulm or debris choking the plant; the 'crown' of the plant imbedded too deeply in the soil; not enough room for the plant to unfold; too many snails. If the base of the plant is surrounded locally by black

Fig. 5 Elodea densa

Fig. 6 Bacopa

Fig. 7 Echinodorus

Fig 8 Vallisneria spiralis

More Popular Plants

63

Fig. 9 Nuphar pumila   Fig. 10. Potanogeton Gay

sand, the rest being all right, then hostile nitrites are being produced instead of helpful nitrates and the tank balance is wrong; similarly if a white precipitate powder appears on the leaves in the morning but dissolves during the day, in which case the tank needs more fish, while in the former the tank needs a good clean.

Plants will also tell you their preferences if you will again listen: the lighter the green of their leaves, the more oxygen they tend to give out; a sudden darkening of the leaf colour means the plant is sulking. If the roots are relatively small and the leaves relatively big then the main nourishment comes from these and plenty of top-lighting would be appreciated but over-pruning would not. The more runners the plant sends out, the better it can stand adverse conditions like poor light (will grow in dark corners) or poor soil (will thrive in the beautiful-to-look-at clean tank base), but the more time it needs to establish itself before the runners have extended its sphere.

For plants, too, a part-change of water may help, especially if the water has gone too acid, most prefer the alkaline; chalk or DH, i.e. water hardness, is different, and softer water like rain-water might help. Just a word of caution though: the first shower of rain tends to wash all manner of industrial pollutants down, so please do *not* use that.

Fertilisation of the plants by fish droppings is beneficial; but not excess urine (part change the water but maintain the same temperature); peat is a good artificial fertiliser which most fish also love.

A whole range of quite beautiful imitation plants made of plastics is now more easily available. It excites the fury of some customers and the pleasure of others. Without doubt it is here to stay — such plants look remarkably good, never fade or fail, don't need planting and can be arranged in positions ideal for decoration, but impossible for growth.

CHAPTER TWELVE

BREEDING

Sooner or later you are bound to fall for this fascinating side of the hobby.

In the beginning it is very easy because of the live bearing fish, i.e. those that don't lay eggs but give birth direct to tiny but fully-formed babies: Guppies, Mollies, Swordtails and Platies to name the well-known favourites. These can be so prolific that they spawn without you having ever considered the possibility, let alone having arranged ideal spawning conditions; suddenly, there they are, a shoal of tiny babies — and you're caught. You'll rush round to your nearest aquarium supplier and get baby food . . .

. . . and, a breeding trap. Adult fish tend to eat the fry, the rivers and lakes would be choked otherwise, and the breeding trap acts as a tank floating within your main tank in which the fry can be matured up to size. A false bottom is nearly always fitted so that the female does not eat her own fry before you can get to save them. The usual time of spawning is often at first light of daybreak. A gravid female can have anything from one or two at a time to over fifty, the usual being around ten or twenty; not unknown are several bursts of deliveries spaced hours, days or even weeks apart.

The future fry are folded head to tail inside the yolk sac of their mother causing on obvious swelling, and, as delivery time approaches, a darkening as the eyes inside become formed and prominent. The young are usually born with a supply of food tending to 'double them up'; as the food is consumed so do they straighten and begin a seemingly endless quest for food.

The gestation period varies with the time of the year, but is quickest in the main season, i.e. spring, summer, autumn; each producing one spawning. However, all manner of factors can influence the time either way — food, water consistency, depth, temperature, over-crowding, nervous disorders, etc. The more nervous the fish, like the female Molly, the more uneven the period, and the more possible the miscarriage or the still-born.

For the first few weeks, all fry including those hatched from eggs, are very susceptible to almost everything, and you can be quite sure that something is wrong if the shoal grows unevenly. Did you switch to bigger foods too soon, or too late? Were there cold draughts, fry often hiding at top water under a floating leaf? Was the water surface clear of scum; was the depth too great, or even too shallow? Temperature variations, sufficient hiding places, pH and DH of water, its clean-liness . . . were all these points satisfactory?

For instance, spawning under ideal conditions is often arranged in a separate thoroughly-sterilised tank of only 45cm × 25cm × 25cm (18in × 10in × 10in) size with perhaps only 15cm (6in) of water depth; this depth being increased by 2.5cm (1in) per week as the fry grow. Soon they will have reached the capacity of the tank, and during the next month should be transferred to a larger one 60cm × 30cm × 30cm (24in × 12in × 12in) or more. Also, the original spawning water will have been scrupulously clean and of a chosen pH and DH, i.e. a chosen degree of acid or alkaline, and of hardness or softness. It may well get fouled, and when replaced should be of the same pH and DH, and this should be done gradually, a little at a time, to avoid fluctuations, including those of temperature and of depth.

Young parents are clearly preferable. It sometimes appears that a female is full of roe, but has in fact merely got a middle-aged spread. It may happen too that your fish refuse to spawn for long periods; clearly, then, something is wrong, and more detailed guidance should be sought as the subject is too big for here. Just as an illustration, the Neons and the Cardinals needed subdued light with strong occasional shafts of penetrating brilliance and their eggs were best hatched in utter darkness maintained for five full days.

Sexing the fish, their optimum requirements for pH and DH, for temperature, foods, conditions and seasons; the period for hatching the eggs, often 24 to 48 hours at 24°C (75°F), but varying with the species, plant requirements, degree of bacteria control, foods and feeding; all need consideration. The enthusiast can really let himself go, as so very many do, because it is such fun.

CHAPTER THIRTEEN

WATER

Of course it's vital to the fish, and, of course, they would be very sensitive to changes in its composition and they would plead with you please to keep it fresh and clean.

As is well known, fish use the mechanism sheltered behind their gill plates to extract the 'goodness' out of the water and to eliminate the noxious waste elements of their own body circulation. If this very delicate and finely adjusted mechanism is damaged, say by shock, for even an hour or two, the fish could literally 'bleed' to death — either because the membranes of the 'intake' side were paralysed and no oxygen plus beneficial salts and trace-elements were being absorbed; or because the 'retaining' side was letting out from the fish not only wastes but the beneficial trace-elements which should have been kept and without which the fish just can't live. An otherwise perfectly healthy fish can die in an hour because its gill plates are temporarily paralysed by shock.

Shock is the key. In their natural habitat fish are never taken from one water and abruptly put in another, to leave one river and jump into another! They just have no protection against this form of sudden change which man imposes on them when he puts them in one tank from another, or flies them from the Amazon to London.

Given the minimum of understanding help, fish will quickly acclimatize themselves to a quite radical change, provided it is done gradually. Gradually! For example, in the wild fish are continually adapting themselves to huge seasonal water changes; when the monsoons swell the rivers and wash down vast quantities of soil, debris, vegetation and so forth, or when the dry heat of the drought shrinks the pool or the stream to relatively little water saturated in decayed vegetation. But these happen slowly.

Fluoride and chlorine are two of the worst of the fish enemies, as both will paralyse the gill plate mechanism. Fluoride has long been known deeply to affect the nerves; put in water it is regularly used to tame wild animals, to make them docile; it was so used in the wartime concentration camps to keep the inmates amenable; it is also thus used in prisons and it is the same stuff some governments are insisting on introducing into the drinking water because of some talk of saving milk teeth. The effect of fluoride on fish is markedly adverse, and you may have difficulty if it is in your tap water. Neither boiling nor filtering will remove it. We do sell tablets which temporarily modify the effects but they're not perfect.

Chlorine is far easier to eliminate from the tap water. Just shaking and frothing it about would do, left in an open-aired tank the chlorine escapes out in a few hours, or tablets are readily available capable of dissipating it in minutes.

Removal of fluoride and chlorine — both artificially introduced by man — merely puts the water back to normal, as it were, but does not make it necessarily healthy for fish. Your tank water is the fish universal provider, its supermarket; everything it needs has to come from there, and you make changes by giving food, or by cleaning out the debris. So the fish supermarket must have a good selection of beneficial trace elements, vitamins, salts, bacteria, etc., and a minimum of hostile nitrites, for example, in the sort of stinking bog of a mess that some people laughingly pass off as an aquarium.

A whole new science of ecology has grown up as this problem of the fish supermarket has been increasingly studied. A total balance of all factors is needed, alter any one of them and all the others are affected in some measure; and, of course, the pH and DH.

PH measures the degree of acid or alkaline in the water; 7.0 being the neutral point, 6.0 being acid and 8.0 being alkaline. Many branded kits are sold to help you measure and alter the pH of the water, but the do-it-yourself aquarists use phosphoric acid or heavily diluted hydrochloric acid to change to more acid; and bicarbonate of soda to do the reverse. Others deliberately introduce peat or other such 'natural' products the more slowly and permanently to make the water acid, and there is much to be said for this.

DH, or degree of hardness, is now far more understood than it was even a few years ago, largely thanks to the German aquarists who consistently studied this aspect and have amply proved its importance. Many many kits are commercially available to help you soften the hard water of London (some 18 degrees) to a DH of only 4 or 8 that many tropical fish prefer, and in which they spawn more readily.

In earlier books and articles I have placed stress on the fact that the water need never be changed in a modern fish tank. Nor need it, but the contrast was often being made with the archaic goldfish-in-a-bowl where the water was constantly discolouring and the fish dying because the fish was consuming the oxygen quicker than the air surface of the water was replacing it. This problem was solved in those earlier books when it was realised that a goldfish was totally unsuitable because (a) it grew too large — 35cm (14in) or more — and (b) needed so much room for swimming and consumed so much oxygen that an outdoor pond, not a bowl, was essential. People had previously been fooled just because the goldfish was so tough that it had lingered on alive in its cramped prison for a few years (or months or days!) stunted in growth and suffering in slow suffocation; in a pond it would otherwise have grown far larger and have thrived for twenty or thirty years. When the (relatively large) goldfish was replaced by the (relatively small) tropical fish, and the bowl (with a small air surface) by a tank (with a large surface) the need for constant changes of water was overcome. The tank could now be balanced, and remain healthy for years.

The new science of ecology, or study of water conditions, has taken us all a big step forward. For example, the DH, or hardness of water, just discussed one paragraph earlier. Tests began to reveal the intricate interplay of many different factors: suppose an all-over top-light had not been fitted, or that there was a marked temperature difference between the tank water and the ambient air, both of which factors would tend to cause the tank water to evaporate abnormally fast; and suppose 10 per cent of the water evaporated each week, and you just topped up with new water — tests showed that in one single month you could almost triple the DH, or hardness of the water! No wonder some aquarists insisted on changing all the water at the slightest excuse. But this act of despair is easily overcome with knowledge, and a balanced healthy tank is the rule, not the exception.

However, all factors need to be considered as a whole: the top-lighting, its type, intensity, duration, and angle of penetration; the plants, in their abundance and their strength; the planting medium and its bacteria forming tendencies; the number and size of the fish and the oxygen they consume and the carbon dioxide they exhale, together with their urine and their waste products. Hence the importance of the size of the tank and its cleanliness. The higher the temperature, the faster the 'rate of the cycle', and the quicker the manifestation of the result of a disturbance of the balance. And, of course, the foods you introduce, smells or toxic fumes in the air, sudden bursts of strong sunlight (millions of candle power) striking the tank, a clogged up filter that pours back dirty water, even poisoned water . . . all these should be considered as a whole.

The bigger the volume of water, with healthy abundant plants, and the greater the rate of flow or circulation of the water, say through a (clean) filter, the more stable the tank balance. Cramming a quart into a pint pot usually brings problems.

CHAPTER FOURTEEN

TROUBLE

If fish fall sick or die there will be a cause that usually can be found and remedied; it may lie with the dealer, with you, with the fish itself, with the tank, or with the room surrounding the tank.

The dealer is assumed to be a specialist who knows his job, who keeps up with the latest medicines and who loves his fish. Such a paragon is as rare as is the perfect customer. Many a dealer is in the game just for the money; his customer is urging him to produce the goods cheaply, and both, therefore, tend to 'cut the safety factors' and so kill or weaken the fish. This is a blunt truth, becoming more so every day.

The ideal dealer will always acclimatize his imports from abroad before sale. Now this item is by far and away the most expensive of the safety factors, and the one most easily reduced — the fish 'looks fine' at the time of sale. To quarantine it longer puts up the price. Would you pay this?

Artificially bred fish now predominate over wild specimens, whether the breeding is done locally, say in Europe, or more usually in the country of origin where the climate makes (expensive) artificial heating unnecessary, and where large outdoor breeding ponds can replace small indoor tanks. But the commercial pressure to 'force-breed' is the same, i.e. to produce too many, too quickly by artificial methods of developing size at the expense of stamina. If it 'looks good' at the time of sale, and is cheap, it sells. It may also be weak, but who would pay 'the extra'? After all fish are so plentiful, so inexpensive, so easily replaced, that few of us humans spare a compassionate thought for their sufferings in force-bred conditions.

Ideally, the dealer's tanks, and your own, should be clean, never overcrowded, and big. This gives a 'poor display' with 'only a few fish in each tank', and many an undiscerning customer walks away because the dealer 'is low on stock today'. So the dealer tends to fill up, the customer tends to buy, and the poor fish tends to die. In Chapter 4 the optimum number of fish that can be kept in a tank has been discussed.

As this ever-growing hobby of tropical fish continues to become more and more commercially important, orthodox medical science becomes further involved in it, resulting in a stream of patent medicines for fish. Most of these are excellent, as for white spot or for fungus, for example.

White spot used to be a real killer before the middle of the century. Then it got tamed by methylene blue, quinine or even sodium chloride, until the increase of atomic radiation caused mutations. The two 'normal' types of white spot mutated to five distinct strains, one of which was virtually incurable, and the disease began to be more and more widespread among the indigenous wild stocks of Asia, Africa and Latin America. In the late 1960-70 decade the position became almost desperate. Then came the spate of 'instant' cures as carefully controlled amounts of ultra-strong chemicals began to be marketed and enabled both the dealer and the customer rapidly to cure affected fish without having to remove them from the community tank. Malachite green was a typical medicine in a dosage of 1.25 drops per 4.5 litres (1 gallon), using a 2 per cent solution made with distilled water. It did not colour the tank water, did not harm too much the plants or other fish, cured in 12-72 hours without having to raise the temperature, and needed only to have the tank water half changed at the finish.

Similarly with fungus: the new drug phenexotol being typical of the many new ones which effected rapid cures without temperature changes and without removing the sick fish from the tank. Even more important, whole outdoor ponds could now be treated because a subsequent water change, after the cure, became less imperative.

General 'cure-all' and 'preventative' medicines have naturally become fashionable; many are pure wishful thinking, some are more modest in their claims and are helpful.

A new attitude to disease is clearly emerging, as people tend to worry less and less about it, and more and more rely on patented medicines. Dealers are not slow to notice this, and fish condition at time of sale becomes more and more problematical. After all, they're cheap; and not too much attention is really paid to how the fish themselves feel.

A positive advance has been made in the understanding of pH and DH (Chapter 13), on water ecology (Chapter 13) and on filtration (Chapter 4) which will all help you in tracing reasons for the death or sickness of fish in your care.

So, too, will attention to psychological fish-needs like open spaces, lighting and hiding places (Chapter 6), changed foods and balanced diets (Chapter 10), and general tank conditions of plants (Chapter 11) and cleanliness. If your water goes green, then you know from Chapter 5 that you are giving the aquarium too much light, be it artificial, natural, or a combination

Rosy Barbs

Tiger Barbs

Black Widow

Dwarf Gourami

Pearl Gourami

Harlequin Fish

Kuhli Loach

Penguin Fish

Platies

P. Plecostomus

Zebra Danios

Pterophyllum Scalare

Scatophagus Argus

Barbus Schuberti

Chilodus Punctatus

of the two, and that trouble may develop if conditions get prolonged or aggravated.

So too with dirt and mulm, *including* that hidden beneath the undergravel filter even though the top sand still looks clean. Tell-tale signs like patches of black sand round the roots of the plants, like fish going discoloured, with drooping fins; listlessness; hanging head down/up; frightened, frantic darts into unaccustomed places; hiding head-first into sand or plant thickets; accelerated breathing with or without swollen or reddened gill plates. All these are signs shrieking at you to clean the tank, or at least to part-change the water, at once. But, at once as minutes count. Please don't overlook the filter, it's almost certainly filthy and saturated.

Less violent symptoms are when fish begin to mope, to splinter off from the group and sulk, go off food, get ragged at the fins, show body blemishes; or white precipitate forms on the plants, often in the mornings; or the plants straggle, the bottom of the stems becoming bare stalks; unusual bubbles of air begin to settle or to colonise on the surface; all these are the beginning of trouble. Have you got a scum, that oily scum of Chapter 4? Are toxic fumes being sucked into your tank, by the air pump for instance? Is your proportion of plants to fish to top-lighting correct? Is the fish diet too monotonous? Is there temperature stratification, i.e. layers of warm water above and cold water below (Chapter 3)? PH and DH? Too much fish urine accumulated? Anything been dropped in? Sure? Have you used cloths or tools or jam jars that smelt or had grease/detergents/polish, etc., on them? How about the temperature at 2 a.m. when the room is cold and the fire is out? When did you last clean the tank?

If the fish keeps its mouth open for unduly long periods, or has scores and swellings or abnormal markings

77

from within which are shown on the outside (as distinct from bangs from without — in) then there is probably internal trouble, usually local to one fish. It can be food that has got stuck, or internal virus or even worms and parasites. Food previously soaked in medicines, might help; so too should your specialist dealer.

Long thread-like exretia hanging from the vent is merely constipation. Some aquarists are for ever adding Epsom salts; others prefer to give more laxative foods like live daphnia, or those with strong vegetable contents. Or was the real cause of the constipation deeper, which built up gradually over a period of time finally showing through in that form (and even in some other). Was it too strong a glaring toplight, relentlessly beating down, with no possibility of shade? Lack of privacy or refuge for a weak or old fish? Loneliness? Fish like a mate, too. Or, have you been neglecting your fish tank lately, causing them to miss you, and feel unwanted!

Diseases
In the wild fish seldom fall sick because free flowing waters and ample space enable most fish to shake off disease; unless man pollutes their waters. Similarly, in your fish tank, your fish will normally stay healthy if your filter system is good enough; ideally your tank waters should be completely filtered every hour — but a clogged-up filter unit, saturated with mulm, will merely serve to pollute, and the faster the turnover the worse the damage — and the ensuing disease.

Medicines should be applied with prudent care. All tank waters differ, the amounts of solids dissolved therein vary, and reactions to the chemicals in the medicine can fluctuate widely. Furthermore, fish vary too; some are allergic, or resistant, to medicines, and

their differing states of health dictate thoughtful adminis-
tration of medicants.

A golden rule is to underdose initially, and see how
your particular tank waters react. Many aquarists give
half-a-dose first; wait a day before adding another
quarter dose; and then wait yet again before adminis-
tering the remaining quarter.

Another golden rule: change, or part change, the
water; before and after treatment. The stronger the
medicine, the more quick-acting, the greater the need to
change the tank water afterwards and replace with waters
warmed to the same temperature.

Softened light, dimmed to darkness even, also helps.
As does special feeding with titbits afterwards, to
hasten recovery.

In short, plain commonsense — just do to your fish
what you would like others to do unto you.

White spot. The most common, for both coldwater
and for tropical fish; distinguished by tiny white spots
the size of a pin-point, rather than a pinhead, scattered
over the fins and body, and often on the head. Each
spot has a normal life cycle of ten to twenty days, the
higher the water temperature the faster the cycle; at
24°C (75°F) a seven to ten day cycle can be anticipated.
On maturity the spot, or cyst as it's known, will drop
off, fragment and actively seek another fish as a host;
dying if it can't find lodgement in twenty-four to thirty-
six hours.

As already stated above, atomic mutations of this
disease now have risen to five (or more) types and one
at least is virtually incurable, although it can be kept
dormant. Being indigenous to open waters of Africa,
Asia, and now of Europe and America, the very act of
taking the fish from one tank and immediately putting

it into another (similar) one, is sufficient of itself to bring on this disease.

Fortunately, many patent medicines are sold that are helpful. Most are based on rapid action ingredients like malachite green, so beware of overdosing. Many of these medicines do not require the water temperature to be raised (useful in the case of outdoor ponds) as used to be the practice.

Fungus. Again prevalent, both for coldwater as for tropicals taking the form of a white cotton-wool growth; often first in the mouth.

Relatively easy to cure with patent medicines or even with common salt: dosage of four days being 2 heaped teaspoons per 4.5 litres (1 gallon) on day one; 2 more on day two; 2 more on day three; leave alone for day four; then change most/all the tank water. Repeat dosage if necessary after a rest of three days.

Shimmies. The fish 'shivers' and 'swims', yet remains rooted to the same spot. Nearly always the cause is bad tank conditions as discussed above in this chapter, demanding correction plus water change.

Dropsy. When the scales stick out giving a bloated appearance. Epsom salts, 2 heaped teaspoons per 4.5 litres (1 gallon), or 30mg of oxtetracycline per 4.5 litres (1 gallon) can be the foundation for a bath of up to three days in such a solution. Please watch for distress if the dose is proving too strong. Change all the water on completion. The exudate from the swollen fish is contagious.

Fin rot / Tail rot. When the red streaks in the fins/tails cause a break-up of tissue, and ends in ragged gaps.

80

Treatment could be the same as for fungus, just described above, and patent medicines usually effect a cure. In extreme cases, the affected parts can be surgically removed (even with sharp scissors).

Bruises, eruptions, blemishes. Each virus has its own particular effects, but general cure-all medicants often help.

Sometimes these visible marks are not caused by blows from without, but from internal disturbances from within: in such cases, the fish food can be soaked in a solution of the chosen medicant, prior to feeding to the fish.

Emergency medicines. If the specialist dealer is not handy, there are several old fashioned stand-by medicines that are easy to administer; available from chemists:
— rock salt: as stated above
— methylene blue (best medical quality): add enough to turn water light blue, blue, darkish blue; stop.
— potassium permanganate: turn water pink, red, darkish red; stop.
— mercurochrome 2% solution: five to ten drops per 4.5 litres (1 gallon). Leave for twelve to twenty-four hours. Watch for distress signs; change most of the water.

Obviously the above are a general guide only, as several medical tomes could scarcely cover all factors. But, most fish do stay healthy, and can be restored if sick. Your specialist dealer is backed by important pharmaceutical firms, and can offer a selection of specially-devised-for-fish medicines that have been laboratory tested.

CHAPTER FIFTEEN

FISH PREFERENCES

Long since passed are the days when a list of two or three hundred names would cover all that you were likely to find in a year's trading. Now it is rare for a single month to pass without a firm new addition to the range.

Gone, too, are all those neat little classifications in genus, family, orders, species and so forth. Renaming and reclassifying fish happens with a frequency and a universality that has left behind all but the most ardent enthusiast; time honoured classifications like platy and swordtail, known to generations are 'no longer valid' — to use technical terms — and have become so blurred in distinction that they are now scientifically useless.

Hence, it is now proposed merely to list in alphabetical order of popular name some typical fish, giving helpful tips on their habits and preferences, to guide the intuitive reader; if you come across a new fish, as surely you will, compare it with the better known ones, seek the points of similarity and thus find the optimum conditions.

For example: the well-known Dwarf Gourami has a small, highly coloured, 'laterally compressed' body, long feelers, bright clear eyes, and a small mouth pointing straight forward, i.e. 'terminal'. Had this been a brand-new fish the above clues would have given a clear index of its preferences:

(1) Small; flat clumsy body; long feelers; small mouth

— obviously no good for attack and safely able to be kept with other fish.

(2) Highly coloured. A perfect camouflage in shallow waters into which pierce blinding shafts of light finding their way through overhanging vegetation — so the fish is accustomed to vegetable-rich waters, i.e. soft waters of low DH say 4–8, and slightly acid of pH 6.8.

The feelers and dainty mouth denote a sensitivity and the clear eyes denote a need for clean waters. The laterally compressed body, unlike a rounded one, indicates a preference for shallowness. Hence, clean, flowing waters, crystal clear, and not too deep are an obvious choice.

(3) The terminal mouth indicating a mid-water swimmer, as distinct from a top swimmer (super terminal) or a bottom grubber (sub-terminal). Add to the clean clear waters, the bright piercing light and the overhanging vegetation, the dainty mouth and you have a mid-water swimmer used to frequent nibbling at plentiful vegetation and algae. A vegetarian fish, by preference.

(4) The defence emphasis of the body, colouring, feelers, etc., strongly suggest group unification as distinct from a lone ranger independence. The fish loves to be in shoals, and is shy to the point of being timid.

(5) Obviously a slow swimmer; therefore, a stay-at-home. The group love to form a protective colony round some (clean) crevices in the rocks, or in thickets of reed-like or bamboo-like plants. Exposed out in the open, and alone, it would wilt.

It may here be worth repeating a short section from an earlier book where this intuitive approach of understanding fish is further discussed:

'Very great guidance and hints for right care are given to you by the fish themselves if you will only look and see. The shape of the fish and the colouring give enormous clues to a loving understanding on your part,

Fig. 11

1 Dorsal Fin	5 Caudal Fin	9 Spiney Anal
2 Spiney Dorsal	6 Pectoral Fin	10 Soft Anal
3 Soft Dorsal	7 Ventral Fin	
4 Adipose Fin	8 Anal Fin	

enabling you to reproduce the more easily the ideal home for your pets.'

The long, slim, torpedo body is obviously intended for fast swimming, and will require open waters. Often this type is light coloured, silvery, streaky, sheeny, all indicating well lit waters, clear and probably fast-flowing. Such fish will love to swim against the tide of the air-pump bubbles, darting into them again and again. Zebras are a good example. All such fish need frequent and lavish feeding.

Very strong colour differentiation on a fish usually means its home waters are overgrown and that strong

84

sunlight penetrates in sharp contrasts of light and shade. The gloriously spectacular living reds and blues of the Neon Tetra and of the Cardinal are perfect camouflage as they glide in and out of the vivid rays of light and dark alternations. The strong stripes of the Tiger Barb, or the heavy mosaic of the Gouramis, indicate similar conditions; the same with striking zig-zag or spots.

Hatchets, Scats, Discus, and the long-feelered Angels or Gouramis have a totally different-shaped body and manifestly require totally different conditions. Almost invisible to look at in front, sideways-on they have a flattened huge body, with a high back, often arching or rounded. Narrow crevices between rocks, through which they can swim in and out are ideal. Please do not have too sharp a turn or corner in the crevices so that the fish fail to navigate through. Yet too wide a channel merely defeats the purpose. Fish will love you for getting it just right. Tall slender plants like *Vallisneria*, in thick clumps with a gap between; or spiky plants in which they can lurk: all would be appreciated.

Most of these with long feelers venture out not too often. Fastidious about cleanliness and food, they prefer to wait for the dainty morsel rather than to guzzle. A complete exception is the Scat (short feelers) which is virtually a scavenger, going anywhere and eating anything. Most fish love to be in a shoal. These laterally compressed, high-bodied ones do so for protection, rather than the sheer joy of swirling numbers shown by the torpedo-shaped zebras. Note, too, the clean-cut vertical markings of the Angels, indicating clear waters, and contrasted with the mix-up of dots and diffused colours of the Scat — a scavenger, that goes anywhere in any water and eats (greedily) off anything.

If the breast fins (the pectorals) are strongly developed, then the fish will probably like to lurk, as just described, but make fast darts out into open clear waters, particularly if its feelers are short or are non-existent. This can apply both to the high-backed flat bodies, and to the torpedo-shaped. Obviously, too, the Hatchet and the Butterfly fish will leap, rather than dart, into the open. Being top-swimmers, they frequently jump into the air, right out of the water, so that their crevices or plants must have a little of a concealed missile launcher about them.

The more arching the back, the more slow the swimmer.

The more flat, or even hollowed, the tummy, the lower down in the water does the fish tend to stay — the catfish has both the arching back and the flat tummy and it lives, as everybody knows, right at the bottom. It shows two further characteristics of bottom dwellers — a dark-coloured back and a pale-coloured tummy — an important clue. Aneus catfish are a good example. Where some others, like the Leopard cats, are lighter in colour, this simply means that its home waters are cleaner, faster-flowing and brighter-lit. You will notice that the tummy of the Leopard cat is still flat and pale, and its back still arches. Of course the upside-down catfish is just being difficult; because it lives upside-down and grubs from the underneath of over-hanging ledges, it has reversed its colouring, but its tummy is distinctly flat, even hollowed.

Eyes are a further clue. Those of the bottom-swimmers are sunken and well spaced apart, indicating the need for shade, or slightly protruding many faceted clear eyes, that seem to look in all directions at once, obviously indicating fast swimmers in open, bright, clean waters. Coupled with gay body-markings you will often find such fish to thrive best in shoals, like the *Hyphessobrycon* Rosaceus or the Serpae. Yet the same high colours of the body denote light and shade, so don't forget some shade, usually a little below water surface but not lower than mid-water.

Mouths are a sure index of the water-levels preferred; superterminal, or pointing upwards, for the top; terminal, or pointing forwards, for mid-water; and sub-terminal, or pointing downwards, for the base-dwellers!

CHAPTER SIXTEEN

SOME POPULAR FISH

In choosing these popular fish no attempt has been made to include all types. Three or four hundred would not have covered the daily commercial range!

Fish have been chosen as typical of very many others:

(a) as to type, and hence as to breeding.

(b) as to shapes, and hence as to their ideal preferences.

This book may well prove to be the first of many approaching the fish with this particular view of 'intuitive understanding', of letting the fish tell us what it likes, of our having 'eyes to see and ears to hear' so that understanding takes place.

Chapter 15 on fish shapes and preferences clearly sets the keynote.

Using this selective technique, you should have far greater success in keeping and in breeding your fish, particularly if you would care to study the fish itself, in your tank, and read the relevant section here at the same time. Quickly you will notice that no attempt whatsoever has been made to do a routine humdrum description, but rather to focus on vital tell-tale points and aspects — the better to understand.

The effort of co-operation required from you is slightly more. But, then, so is the reward.

Some popular fish

ANGEL FISH, originally known as *Pterophyllum eimekei* and *scalare*, are from the Amazon. Now found in ever increasing varieties as these firm favourites are bred all over the world. Veil-tail Angels, Lace Angels of a darker colouring, Black Angels, Lace Veil-tail, Black Veil, Marbled, White, Blue, Blushing, Glass; to name only ten well-known types.

Lovely rounded bodies, denoting preference for deeper waters; clear bright eyes (often rimmed with a striking red) denoting love of brightly lit open spaces; striking well-defined body bands and graceful long feelers, obviously asking for clear waters and clean tanks; thin 'compressed' bodies, which love to 'make a home' in rock crevices or reed clumps and which would incline to sulk or to turn aggressive (in inverted defence) out in the unprotected open, exposed to hurly burly, and devoid of privacy.

The whole body structure suggests: (a) basic shyness, born of evolved sensitivity, that requires a mixture of a 'home' (e.g. a crevice) and open spaces into which they can sail forth, (b) in groups, like a graceful flotilla, secure in their collective numbers.

As you would expect from such advanced-in-evolution fish they require a high standard from you, the owner: clean, soft water of DH 8—12, neutral pH, rich in trace elements. This is the main key. If your local water suits them, they will breed readily.

Fastidious, of course, they will wilt or go on hunger strikes, get ragged fins, mope in corners, if you are failing in providing right waters. They require good and especially varied foods; live foods are particularly welcomed and personal attention from you. The degree to which they can respond to the human voice is flattering.

Temperature tolerance is wide, 22°–24°C (72°–75°F) is excellent. They grow to 15cm (6in) or more, and have those lovely extended dorsal and anal fins that impart such grace and dignity.

Courtship is of the normal chiclid type with rather violent trials of strength through locked jaws and somewhat rough play. Once mated they tend to stay in faithful pairs, and to take great care of the young. Typical of their shy/agressive duality they have been known to eat their eggs or even their fry 'in order to protect them' if their breeding privacy is disturbed.

Dim lighting, clear-flowing aeration, a minimum of chemicals, and the eggs hatch in 48 hours at 24.5°–26.5°C (76°–80°F), growing rapidly in the usual way. Please don't overdo ozonisation.

Two female Angels have been known to pair off and to produce infertile eggs; sexing is not always easy and self-chosen pairs are obviously best. The males have the following characteristics: anal fin sharply angled from the body; pointed genital papilla, angled backwards; protruding lower jaw; slightly more circular body but a bright light shone sideways through the fish shows a flat topped intestine with a depression in it. For the females the following clues will differentiate: straight anal, well developed; rounded genital papilla; examination sideways through a bright light shows a circular intestine, including the top. Distance between ventral and anal fins is relatively great and is straight lined. Viewed head-on the female body is more full behind and below the pectorals.

APHYOSEMION AUSTRALE. Typical of the beautiful 'tooth carps' from West Africa, in gorgeous colours and a 'torpedo-body with appendages'. There is a strangeness, an ultra-colouring, an intensity of feeding and living, a clear impression of being 'forced and pushed' that gives the clue to its home surroundings and, therefore, of its unusual preferences.

It comes in fact from shallow pools and rivulets that form in the tropical rainy season, flourish for a few short hectic weeks, and then dry out. No wonder its colours are intense, as though heightened by fear (of inevitable drought), depicting preference for strong overhead lighting shaded in patches. The fins grow so luxuriously that the waters would have to be shallow and protected. Hence small tanks, only 10cm–23cm (4in–9in) deep are an obvious choice.

Their very definite mouths, super terminal or terminal according to species, denote an intensity in search for food, so that frequent feeding is called for.

It will wilt at once in dirt or in hard water. When the rains come the eggs left buried from the previous year hatch almost straightaway, while the water is still clean, bacteria free, soft, and acid; and the temperature has not yet risen to dry out the pools. Hence, DH 8, pH 6.8, 23°–24.5°C (74°–76°F), and ozonization will help; so, too, will a peat base.

It appears that the eggs cannot hatch by themselves as the outer covering is extra thick to protect them during the long drought. The rains soften the 'peaty' dried vegetation of the previous year, develop the growth of beneficial bacteria, which eat the outer-shell of the eggs, allowing them to hatch. The fry then eat the bacteria and hasten on to mature quickly, mate and spawn before the pool dries out, imprisoning next year's eggs in the mud.

Hence the intensity with which these tooth carps live: can you blame the males for staking out a claim and for fighting off potential rivals, i.e. other males of their own kind. They do not seem to be too interested in others — after all their total life span is only months.

Hatching period for the eggs is dependent on the local circumstances of the pool or rivulet, and hence varies from two to fourteen weeks! The eggs seem easily to get 'frightened', to 'reverse gestation' and to prepare

91

to hold out through a drought till next year. Then, if they 'get their confidence back', they restart gestation and hatch, weeks later. Exactly what causes this 'fright' is difficult to say, but shrinking water depth and increased temperature as the drought approaches are two obvious possibilities. Equally obvious is a decreasing cleanliness of water as debris blows into the newly formed pools and subsequent alteration of ecological factors, notably DH and pH. So an even temperature, clean soft water, constant depth, unaltered lighting, pH, DH, frequent feeding, positively no draughts in the shallow tank (whoever heard of a cold draught of air in African summers?), shady plants, dark peaty base and your *Aphyosemion australe* will thrive and live and play and jump (watch out!) with an intensity you will not forget. That and their beautiful colours make them great favourites.

There are many kinds, of course, blurring one into the other, but still known by their old fashioned names like *Aphyosemion calliurum calliurum, A. calliurum ahli, A. calliurum schmidti* and a whole group of 'non peaceful' ones like *schontedeni, gardneri,* or *elegans.* Basically there are the mid-water types and the bottom-ten-centimetres-of-water types. An obvious clue is the mouth — super terminal (above), terminal (middle) and sub terminal (bottom). The more 'definite' the mouth and the fewer the trailing-flowing fins, the more you need to watch out for attacks on other fish — aphyosemions like eating, fast!

APISTOGRAMMA RAMIREZI. Typical of the 'dwarf chiclids' from Venezuela, and a firm favourite.

Its strong colours, stubby body and snout, relatively big finnage all denote its general peacefulness, though the purposeful appearance of strength indicates that it will stand up for its rights. Particularly when defending its home, the body is obviously not that of a fast, far swimmer, and it is in fact a great home-lover. Give it its own cave, hole or hollow and it will live and let live, merely shooting off intruders.

True to its good colouring it likes strong overhead light penetrating through leafy foliage; clear eyes, denoting clean water; somewhat compressed body denoting shallow depths.

Slightly alkaline pH 7.0 to 7.2, DH 8–10, 23°–24.5°C (74°–76°F) and water depth of 25cm–30cm (10in–12in) soon grow it up to its matured 9cm ($3\frac{1}{2}$in) length. Has a marked preference for cleanliness, green-stuffs, and sand terraces interspersed with rocks, flower pots, caves, arches and so forth.

Not always easy to sex, the female usually has stronger red on her flanks in breeding condition and shows a short genital papilla. But she often takes the spawning initiative and can look very like the male.

Spawning can be induced by a 1°C (2°F) temperature increase, and the adhesive eggs are usually well hidden on previously cleaned rocks or even leaves. 48 hours at 25.5°C (78°F) is usual for hatching and the fry are able to take infusoria, brine shrimps and micro worms in quite rapid progresssion, reaching the stage of eating small daphnia in two weeks. Both parents guard the brood, with the female tending to be the dominating partner.

APISTOGRAMMA AGASSIZI is also famous, with similar characteristics: slightly accentuated, e.g. its finnage is not quite so pronounced, so it is not quite so peaceful. The female is even more bossy than for the *ramirezi* and definitely hen-pecks. Her breeding colour on the flanks is yellow with black spots but even takes on the male colouring in the fins (blue-green with luminous shiny dots) when being particularly assertive. During care of the brood she frequently banishes the male to the outer regions, allowing him to come home only when it suits her.

The eggs may take four days to hatch at 25.5°C (78°F) and often number two hundred.

Both species are fastidious as to conditions, witness their definite body colourations and clear eyes, and are liable to sickness if things are not right. So, too, of course, with the eggs and the fry. Medicines should be used in homoeopathic doses rather than in the more orthodox allopathic, i.e. in very small doses.

BARBS (many of the *Puntius* genus). There are literally dozens upon dozens of different trends of these lively, playful, almost boisterous, fish, and, as an example, let us take the Tiger Barb, scientifically known as *Tetrazona*.

Its clear cut markings, golden sheened body, slightly arched, all suggest clear waters, warm temperatures, nimble movements rather than long swims, bright light, and some definite plant shading. Hidden barbels denote keen interest in food, and lack of pugnacity denotes a preference for shoals.

Liable to hang head (or tail) up if the water is not clean enough, i.e. has too much invisible fish urine or hostile bacteria in it, otherwise they can stand almost anything, anybody, or any food. Often accused of being fin nippers, they tend to play among themselves and to leave others alone provided there is a shoal of at least three or four, and provided hiding places are available as well as open waters.

Being boisterous by nature, so too is their mating which conforms to the normal pattern except that the eggs tend to get scattered in the frenzy. Otherwise the

details are much as described for the *Rasbora*, although
the Barbs are not as fussy over the water. DH 8—12,
pH 7.0, 25°—26°C (77°—79°F), and well oxygenated
tanks suit them very well.

The older the fish, the more the body arching becomes
pronounced; in case of general listlessness, a change of
water and a lowering of DH from 8—12 to 4—6 is almost
certain to help. Usual length 5cm (2in).

Rosy Barb (*Barbus conchonius*) was one of the
original imports, and is still in demand, though its
larger size of 9cm (3½in) and its relatively drab colours
have lessened this. The high colouring 'rosy' of its name
happens only in breeding condition.

Its drab 'sluggish' colours indicate its capacity to
stand lower temperatures — down to 15.5°C (60°F) —
and is tough enough to survive adverse treatment.

Golden Schuberti Barb is a descriptive name that
still sticks although scientifically it is 'no longer valid',
having been merged with *Barbus semifasciolatus*,
amongst others.

Its relatively quiet colouring indicates its indifference
to temperature, and it will breed at only 22°—23°C
(72°—74°F) or less. Undemanding, it is easily spawned
and reared and hence is still a favourite. Length 10cm
(4in), peaceful, unobtrusive, and adaptable.

Our three examples have focused on the boisterous
and the quiet, the colourful and the plain, the large and
the small. In a genus where there are hundreds of types,
such variety is to be expected.

Betta Splendens (Siamese Fighting Fish). One of the
most famous of them all. By now most people realise
that these can safely be kept in a community tank,

although not with another male of their own species, and, also, not usually with a female lest they start protecting (or hating!) her and causing trouble all round.

Magnificent finnage; ever improving with new strains, some transparent, some coloured, some shot and flecked. In gorgeous colour sheens; pure or mixed, with red, blue, green and albino predominating; but by no means being exhaustive. Growing to a sturdy 7.5cm (3in), these dominating males are short-lived, thirty months or less, and ride rough-shod over their terrified females who are shorter finned, paler, smaller, and no match whatsoever for their vigorous partners.

The long torpedo body indicates swift movement, but is too encumbered with (beautiful) finnage to allow for long swims, and the fish is a real stay-at-home; in fact, this can only too readily develop into sulks in corners if conditions don't suit it. The flaring gill plates and imposingly extending fins preclude gregariousness, with others of its type, but a lofty disdain of lesser breeds. High colouring points to its preference for warmer, clean waters of 25°–29°C (77°–84°F). The business-like mouth will tackle most foods, but would scorn the unworthy. Algae is also taken willingly as its superb colouring surely indicates bright waters heavy with growing plants. Obviously, it is a lurker rather than a wanderer, and needs a 'home' of its own.

Having an auxiliary breathing apparatus, it periodically surfaces to gulp air, and is therefore very tolerant of water conditions. This labyrinth breathing makes understandable its breeding characteristics: a floating nest of air bubbles, coated with saliva and anchored where surface plants and algae abound, is used to house the eggs. Constantly the burst bubbles are more than replaced, usually by the male alone, and any fallen eggs replaced in the nest whose increasing thickness lifts the eggs more and more until they are clearly visible from the top. They are very sensitive indeed at this stage to cold draughts or to dust and to oily scum.

When hatched the fry hang vertically from the nest, wriggling back to position if dislodged, but start swimming vertically after a few days if infusoria food has been plentiful. Up till now, the male is usually very protective of the brood, but directly this begins to break up and they swim independently he should be removed.

Water level can be kept down to 10–15cm (4–6in) during breeding, being gradually increased the usual 2.5cm (1in) per week. Sunlight, periodic water changes to help remove some of the over abundant foods usually demanded and, to repeat, no draughts, oil or dust, will help ensure good results. Water can be DH 4–6, pH 6.8–7.0, seasoned with peat, and kept at 25.5°–28°C (78°–82°F).

Males are very fussy about the females they accept, and their courtship is rough in the extreme. It is essential to condition up the female separately, introduce her gradually to the male, say for an hour at a time separated off in a jar or by a partition, before putting them together in the prepared tank during late evening. The female may need protection if she does not please or is not in sufficiently full spawning form; otherwise mating could easily start in the early morning. The exhausted female should be removed as soon as it is over.

Grown fry of almost three months can still be kept together because sex differentiations and finnage have not yet developed. At a body length of 2.5cm (1in) the male anal fin begins to incline obliquely downward; staying parallel to the body in the female. Separation time is rapidly approaching.

BLACK WIDOW (*Gymnocorymbus ternetzi*). Paraguay. Length 6cm ($2\frac{1}{2}$in). A good old oldie that every aquarist

97

seems to have kept since the early part of this century. Its clear, neatly defined, contrasting black markings on a silver green sheened body, its bright, red rimmed eyes, all show its need for clear waters, well lit, with strongly growing foliage interspersed with open spaces. A firm super terminal mouth shows its self-confidence, its ability to look after itself, yet not aggressive enough to be pugnacious; the fish gets on well with others, and is also happy in a shoal.

Its laterally compressed body, fairly rounded, indicates a mid-water, fastish swimmer, tending to go to top waters in search of food since the mouth is super terminal. It has a certain restlessness and mobility that lessen the need for a 'home'.

Males have the usual characteristic of Characins, i.e. a hooked anal fin. Also as usual the more humped the body, the older the fish. Fading colours also indicate old age, although these can be brought on, of course by adverse conditions or by fright.

Easy to keep and spawn, the eggs are free-scattered and hatch in 48 hours, they are adaptable but will thrive at DH 6–8, pH 6.8, 25.5°–26.5°C (78°–80°F). They love dancing aeration and will dive and play in the bubbles. To rest they often hang motionless under a shady leaf, going pale as they sleep. Sensitive to foul waters they protest by going off balance and hanging head down, patiently waiting for you to part change the water. They will eat almost any reasonable foods, preferring flesh to vegetables.

New varieties now have truly magnificent veil tailing fins, which are strikingly graceful and taut, and yet maintain their strong black colouring.

CARDINALS (*Cheirodon axelrodi*). Length 7cm (2$\frac{3}{4}$in). Rio Negro. Breathtaking in its beauty, with the 'living colours shining from within—out'; a wide luminous red band the full length from the mouth through the eye, to the caudal peduncle; bordered below with a phosphorescent red band from the gills to the tail. It has displaced the world renowned Neon tetra for beauty, and is slightly larger as well; although the two are similar.

Their intense 'living' colours are perfect camouflage in shallow heavily overgrown waters, pierced by blinding shafts of strong sunlight, and give strong hints to their home requirements. Clean, clear, soft waters; flowing over and through heavy vegetation, hence acid; warm; and not too deep, open spaces bordered by sheltering thickets.

Cardinals come in fact from the overhung rivulets of the head waters of the mighty Rio Negro where the emerging waters are clean, pure and 'bacteria-free', i.e. DH 2—4, pH 6.5—6.8, peat covered base, dark in colour, 24°—28°C (75°—82°F), depth 30cm (12in) or so.

The male is slimmer, less rounded, and his green line is more straight. A strong light shone sideways shows a swim bladder tapering towards the tail, leaving a free space between the bladder and the viscera. The female bladder is rounded and the free space is filled by the ovary. Young adults are obviously best for breeding and should be allowed to pair off naturally, being conditioned up till their colours are intense, using, for example, chopped up white worms, brine shrimp eggs, tubifex and daphnia. September/October and April/May are good breeding times.

Absolute cleanliness is the rule. The 46cm X 25cm X 25cm (18in X 10in X 10in) breeding tank with spawning mops or soft plants, absolutely should have been sterilised; filled to 15cm (6in) or so with water as already described, leaving plenty of free swimming space round the mops or plants; and, last but by no means least,

99

allowing strong exterior-to-the-tank side lighting (not overhead) to filter through translucent green paper.

As is usual the separately conditioned female is introduced first, and the male at dusk. Sometimes spawning follows automatically next morning, sometimes not. In which case, alter the temperature 1°C (2°F), the water depth 2.5cm (1in), reposition/reduce/increase the mops, recheck for cleanliness; is the base covering of peat enough; did you use previously-soaked-in-peat water; try aeration; is the light too dim/strong or not diffused/streaky enough? One or more of these factors is almost certain to work.

Rapid darts into the thickets start the spawning, which get more frenzied, side by side, quivering and touching − and scattering the semi-adhesive eggs. Those lost at the bottom are more likely to be attacked by bacteria than the ones protected by the sterilised mops or plants. Three hours is usually enough, and the parents can be removed.

Fear of bacteria is the next main hurdle, and complete and total darkness should now envelope the tank for five full days. A mild disinfectant of methylene blue or of acriflavine may help, so, too, does very gentle aeration, and a temperature of 24°−25.5°C (75°−78°F).

During the darkness the eggs should hatch in forty-eight hours, live off their yolk sacs, and be free swimming (and starvingly hungry!) when the light is progressively restored after five days. Frequent feeding on newly hatched brine shrimps, and growth is rapid.

The fear of bacteria, heightened by the frequent feeding, causes some breeders to transfer the growing fry to new tanks (of identical waters) rather than merely part change the waters. Of course, the water depth is increased 2.5cm (1in) a week, up to say 30cm (12in).

The NEON TETRA (*Hyphessobrycon innesi*) are similar, and slightly smaller. They come from more or less the same types of rivulets as the Cardinals, and can be kept and bred as just described.

Both are hardy, peaceful, and beautiful; looking best in shoals of six or more, viewed by side lighting obliquely across a dark base.

The golden GLOW LIGHT TETRA (*Hyphessobrycon gracilis*) also qualifies with its intense gold stripe, shining from within-out, and has almost identical requirements. Except that it is slightly less fastidious, and can stand another 1°−1.5°C (2°−3°F) of temperature, tending to feel the cold more than the other two.

DISCUS *Symphysodon* (original red), *Symphysodon aequifasciata haraldi* (Blue Discus), *Symphysodon aequifasciata axelrodi* (normal Brown Discus), *Symphysodon aequifasciata aequifasciata* (Green Discus) to mention but a few of the names of but a few of the types of this new 'Queen of the Aquarium', positively the favourite of favourites. Scarcely known before 1957!

Its shape gives a clear index of its ideal requirements: beautiful circular body, laterally compressed, and free of distortions − deep tanks essential; rock crevices, reed hide-outs, a nice home of its own, obviously a must; perfect symmetry, hence highly evolved, hence expects a high standard from you, and just anything will not do! Short feelers, often coloured; fastidious, to be sure, proper foods must be properly served. Clear, red-rimmed eyes and mosaic of high colours: clean, well-lit waters, lavishly sheltered by plants and rocks, flowering through and over lush vegetation with strong lights beating through in alternating light/shade patterns; warm. Defensive rather than aggressive: hence shy, a stay-at-home, gregarious; pine when alone and neglected,

101

flourish in a shoal, and respond readily to your love and affection. Will know your voice; will miss you and mope when you are absent. Tameable and lovable. A true 'queen of the fish tank', requiring regal, roomy quarters. Not to be cramped into a bed-sitter! DH2–4, pH 6.8, 24.5°–29°C (76°–84°F), clean; filtered.

Yet Discus are adaptable, increasingly so as many strains are being widely bred in captivity; the colours shade, merge and alter according to local conditions and moods. A light base, mulm, poor lighting, insufficient shade/light contrast, lack of hide-outs, overcrowding and exposure to noisy/flickering/banging hurly burly soon affects their nerves — much more so than poor foods or hard waters.

Mild medicine like Aureomycin ($\frac{1}{4}$ gram per 4.5 litres) can help, so too, can the companionship of the gentle Dwarf Gourami; change of water, rise of temperature, and hand feeding with chopped white worms but done in the immediate vicinity of their home, are well-known stand-bys for difficult periods and moods. A new 'house' built of matured tree-bark; tall, but roofed-in, not too wide apart, but with fairly hidden entrance and a separate exit, is also likely to please. So too will peat.

The male anal fin is more pointed at the end towards the tail, his genital papilla tends also to be pointed, and the ventral fins hang down and then curve backwards in a crescent shape. More bull-headed, his colours are deeper particularly on the head area, and just behind, and in the fins; he is larger in total size. The female genital papilla is cone shaped and rounded off; her ventral fins sweep straight down, curve, and sweep again, to form an 'S' shape, her body bands are slightly less clear-cut, and yellow often predominates over red in her colours but not after spawning takes place when the male, too, seems then to emphasise the yellow.

Separately conditioned parents, can be introduced to the tank which is brightly lit and well planted as already described. A lowering of the light intensity, and a 1°C (2°F) raise of temperature often induces the relatively mild love play, and some 200 adhesive eggs are carefully laid on the cleaned and prepared surface. Often they are laid in neat rows, from above down, and fertilized at the same time. Hatching in forty-eight hours the fry hang on for another two days before becoming free-swimming; laggards are often sucked clear by the solicitous parents.

As you would expect, privacy and freedom from noise, light flashes, or other distractions are essential. Frightened parents have been known to eat their eggs or fry.

Given reasonable conditions the parents are constantly fanning, cleaning, shepherding the unruly brood, and, especially at nightfall when the fry seem to delight in refusing to be adhered to the chosen shelter.

The parents allow the fry to suckle an excretion, or sort of mucus, covering the whole body; one parent in turn acts as 'host' allowing the brood to nibble all over his or her body. At change-over time the relief parent swims alongside, enticing the brood, while the other suddenly darts off. The fry suckle this mucus for very many days, and a 'foster parent', usually a second female, has been introduced to help things along, strange as this may seem. Once the fry are truly free swimming and are eating well, it is relatively rare for them to be attacked by their parents, including 'foster' ones. Newly hatched brine, shrimps, grindal worms, tubifex 'pre-chewed' by the parents, and sifted live daphnia are all taken.

Once the fry grow to 2.5cm (1in), usually in a week, the parents should be removed. Relatively frequent part-changes of water, help develop the disc shape in about twelve weeks; sexual maturity takes another twenty months.

DWARF GOURAMI (*Colisa lalia*). India. Length 5.75cm ($2\frac{1}{4}$in). In Chapter 15 the ideal preferences of this delightful and truly beautiful fish have already been detailed. So too have its breeding habits, which are standard for the labyrinth breathers or anabantids, as described for the *Betta splendens*, except that the male is not brutal.

Very sensitive to water depth (an alteration of even a couple of centimetres can affect it), to cleanliness of water, and to draught-free warmth.

The male dorsal fin in definitely larger, more pointed and, of course more colourful as is his whole body.

DH 4–6, pH 6.8–7.0, 24.5°–29°C (76°–84°F); aeration and heavily planted tanks, cleaned and well lit. Respond favourably to Acriflavine.

Other similar favourites are the Lace Gourami, or Pearl Gourami (*Trichogaster leeri*), growing to a gorgeous 12.5cm (5in), but always staying peaceful. Less striking are the Thick Lipped Gourami (*Colisa labiosa*), growing up to 10cm (4in), and of course, the variations; the Honey, the Croaking, the Kissing, the Chocolate, the Marmarota, the Opaline and the Jewel Gouramis to name seven of the more popular. Beware of 'Three-spot' or Blue Gourami which definitely can be pugnacious.

All these fish eat Hydra, and will soon clear an affected tank if given no other foods.

ELEPHANT NOSE. Mormyrids. Upper Nile. 12.5cm (5in). A quaint lovable fish that has got itself a bad name, mostly undeserved. Basically it is ultra-shy, ultra-frightened and, therefore, 'appears aggressive' in exaggerated self-defence. Just give it a home of its own where it can feel safe and secure, and it will watch the world go by, staying peacefully in its immediate area and bothering no one. In fact, it won't even leave the home area for food, and will starve if not fed there. This applies to each Elephant Nose you keep; two specimens will need two, preferably three quite separate hide-outs; the third 'spare' one helps each to feel more secure in the one it's got. Even spawning pairs demand this, before and after the acts.

The whole appearance of the fish bears out the above remarks — obviously not good for attack, clumsy body, tiny mouth at the end of its elephant-like trunk; its sole real defence is to be able to emit a mild electric shock, too weak to harm but just enough to afford some protection.

Thickly embedded eyes and drab colouring clearly mark it out to be a bottom grubber, in mud, silt, decaying vegetation, mulm, etc; and obviously in dim light. Hopelessly inadequate to cope with fast-flowing movement in open bright areas they will hide all day in such conditions and come out only at night, dusk and dawn. Yet given a soft, dark coloured bottomed tank, set up as indicated, full of nooks and crannies of old flower pots, caves, arches and tree bark; lit with diffused, slightly murky light; and they will play all day long in and around the home, tossing a leaf like a beach ball. Once tamed to the sound of your voice they will hang on your every word, and positively will wilt if you then neglect them — their security will have been shattered.

As you would expect from the dainty mouth the fish are personally clean, and will keep their home thus; nor too, will they eat any old foods. Most clean small morsels are acceptable, usually picked up 'from above' off the ground; they do not seem to like to have to 'reach up' for it, and, of course, won't leave the home area. Food

105

particles are sucked in, rather than chewed (although there are a few teeth) and need to be appropriate in size and texture.

DH 4–10, pH 6.2–7.0, 24.5°–26.5°C (76°–80°F). Many varieties exist, with long and short trunks, and some with really pleasant markings. Sizes vary too.

HARLEQUIN (*Rasbora Heteromorpha*). Length 4.5cm (1$\frac{3}{4}$in). Typical of many of its genus that come from the Malayan archipelago. Included here partly because it's a good old favourite, beautiful and hardy, and partly because of the ever growing fashion of keeping only small-growing fish; genuinely tiny jewels; in small, separate tanks, neatly matched in patterns, tiers or rows.

The body markings are not a mosaic of various colours, but clearly are grouped in one definite triangle on relatively a plain background; the background being clean and reflective; all of which suggests a love of brightly lit open spaces (look at its featured red-rimmed eyes), clean, clear waters, not particularly overgrown or shaded. Its body is medium-slim, tending to a balanced top plus below arching, indicating a medium swimmer, and, lacking offensive characteristics, tending to be gregarious and preferring to be in shoals. So it needs open swimming space, but not too much or too violent, i.e. not a strong current for instance, a backwater rather than midstream. Medium depth of water is also suggested.

In fact, the fish comes from clean, gently flowing shallow creeks carpeted by sand-cum-fallen vegetation. The waters are extremely soft, right down to DH 2, and this is one main factor for its health and for breeding.

It likes high temperatures as may be guessed from its body sheening, well-formed scales, and nimble movements; nothing sluggish or cold about a *Rasbora*.

Eating most foods readily — it lacks the fastidiousness

106

of long feelers, or the greed of short barbels — it can be conditioned up for spawning, using DH 2—4, pH 5.5 to 6.0, 24°C (75°F), clean sandy base covered with some peat or cryptocorine leaves, the spawning act can be induced by raising the temperature 1.5°—3°C (3°—5°F) in a thoroughly sterilised tank.

The male colourings are greater, including the red of the eye, and the lower tip of the triangular wedge is slightly forward reaching. It is slimmer than the female, whose plumpness round the base of the triangle shows especially from above, and causes a slight blurring of the markings. The gold colour seems to predominate in the female, rather than the red of the male.

The spawning act itself is normal, the pair staying quietly in mid-water or under a protective ledge or leaf until one (usually the female) takes the initiative to start the frenzied spawning chase enticing the partner over the chosen thicket. Then, motionless quivering, upside down, brushing the chosen thicket or leaf with the vent, the male clasps the female wrapping his tail round her, to squeeze out a dozen or so adhesive eggs at each embrace; repeating the chase and embrace until nearly two hundred eggs can have been extruded and the female is exhausted.

The parents removed, great care now has to be taken to protect the eggs from disease, although the tank had previously been sterilised. Many breeders keep the tank in darkness for five days; some add mild chemicals like methylene blue. Hatching in 24-26 hours, the fry are free swimming in another five days. The water depth can now be increased 2.5cm (1in) per week, and the DH gradually brought up to a more normal 8—10. In passing it could be noted that the extreme softness of DH 2 suggested above is for wild specimens straight from Malaysia. Tank bred specimens abound, and these have been kept and bred in all kinds of water.

Other firm *Rasbora* favourites are *maculata* or *uropthalmus* for the smaller ones and many larger varieties like *trilineata, einthoveni, pauciperforata*, etc. Naturally these distinctions are less clear cut than they used to be, and new types are regularly coming forth.

HEADSTANDERS *Chilodus Punctatus*. Guyana. Length 7.5cm (3in). Typical of the fish that do not float on an even keel, these stay head down.

The pronounced arch of the back, the small terminal mouth (which has small teeth behind the lips), the general slow-moving carriage, and the slightly 'piercing' eyes give a clue to its preferences. Not too much open space with attendant rough and tumble; hence a 'live and let live' type. A nibbler, it might even have degenerated into a scavenger but for the dainty mouth, constantly requiring to peck at food. Its drab colours suggest drab not-too-clean places — tangled, overgrown thickets round falled branches and twigs suit it fine. Soft sand, even silted mud, decaying vegetation; all these help it, so too does a humid, oppressive sort of swampy warmth, and cold draughts would certainly not be welcome any more than would be swift water flow. It loves algae, and hiding places.

DH 6, pH 6.6, 25.5°–30°C (78°–86°F), are suggested although its tolerance is wide, provided the temperature is kept high.

Of course, there are many variations on this old standing favourite, that tolerates dirty water, even accentuating its rather drab colours therein.

Relatively easy to spawn, it helps to have the top lighting raised well above water surface and focused to alternate between strong penetration and diffused straggle. Some 150 eggs hatch in three days at 26.5°–

29°C (80°–84°F) and are free swimming in a week; an increase to 30°–31°C (86°–88°F) helps. The parents are not particularly solicitous and should be removed after spawning. Draughts are fatal, as already stressed.

KHULI EELS. (*Acantopthalmus kuhlü*). Length 9cm ($3\frac{1}{2}$in). Typical of the ever-increasing number of eels now imported, with varying markings, thickness and lengths. Peaceful and industrious, they are largely dark or dusk (i.e. half light) enthusiasts, and tend to hide away in bright lights. They entwine round plants, jam in between rocks, literally burrow into the sand, yet can swim at a fantastic speed if disturbed. This is what really keeps them from being even more popular; they are so fast that dealers hate having to catch them, at the cost of a wrecked tank decor.

Obviously they like burrowing and rummaging among decayed vegetation, mulm, twigs, reed-like plants, thick-stemmed sturdy ones, old flower pots, rock caves, and so on. A bare tank is hopeless for them. The eyes are covered by a transparent skin, for protection, as they wriggle through the most unlikely places and indicate that they like clean waters, this is important. Gregarious in the extreme, you often find a clustered colony of them hidden in the tiniest of hide-outs. Eat anything that fits their small mouths. When unhappy or frightened they swim restlessly up and down. Given a big enough tank they would move right away from an unpleasant area, yet they are firm home lovers once they have found a niche that suits.

For spawning they leave the accustomed bottom part of the tank, and whirl and frenzy, right at top water, which then must have many branched twigs and, preferably, shady leafed surface clumps for them to love — nuzzle and entwine in. This much we might have guessed

109

from their adaptable, swift, easy movement and freedom from fixed restrictions. The waters should be clean, soft, slightly acid, aerated strongly, and warm; DH 4–8, pH 6.8, 24°–27.5°C (75°–82°F). Muted streaky lighting helps.

PENGUINS (*Thayeri obliqua*). Amazon. Length 8cm ($3\frac{1}{4}$in). As usual, an intuitive look at the fish soon gives an idea of its preferences.

Clean silver-golden sheened body, bright eyes; obviously likes open, clean, well lit waters; particularly in view of the neatly drawn unsmudged, black line transversing the whole length from the eyes to the far tip of the tail.

Yet the appearance is certainly not one of attack; it even lacks a little in confidence. This is accentuated by the peculiar way it always hangs tail-down, when at rest, heightened by the extra long lower fin of the twin-finned tail, with the black line curving down to the furthest and lowest corner. Obviously then it needs the support of a shoal, and will tend to hide among plants if alone.

The slightly super terminal mouth is business-like and the body suggests a fair turn of speed so that undue liberties should not be taken with this fish. Especially the one that has been kept alone, hiding in plants, and getting fretful — such a one has been known to take it out of a weaker fish that approached too near. The mouth, too, also indicates that it prefers to reach up for its food, and would not be too happy at having to leave top-waters to go down to the bottom for sunken particles.

A great favourite; easily kept and spawned. DH 2–4, pH 7.0, 24°–28°C (75°–82°F), aeration, and clean bright waters, frequently changed, suit it well; as do tall, well grown plants.

PIPE FISH (*Syngnathus spicifer*). Ceylon. Length 18cm (7in). Quite distinct from the African varieties which tend to be longer, and which often need salt or brackish water. These relative newcomers from Ceylon also like brackish water but adapt to fresh fairly easily.

Care has to be taken over the food, which has to be taken to the fish, rather than the other way round. Like the Elephant Nose, it too has a small mouth more given to suck than to chew; located as a small opening in a long snout, the lower jaw does hinge, and there is a definite snap action of closure, yet the suck-in-draught still predominates. Even tubifex worms cannot be taken whole, if they are long. Small, sifted live daphnia is ideal (anything too fast would elude this quaint fish) as are pre-mashed morsels of prepared foods, e.g. shrimp, roe, prawn, porridge, finely chopped worms and meat, etc.

About the length and thickness of a commercial pipe cleaner, its body twists and bends according to the mood. A few short jabs of acceleration, a swim with a wavy undulation of the dorsal, otherwise the fish tends to be static, with the occasional slowly unwinding movement. Clearly it needs twigs to perch on, tall, reed-like plants to house in; streaky, murky light; mud-like silt base; clear of decaying vegetation and leaves but furnished with tubes, hollows, clumped twigs, flower pots, etc. DH 8−10, pH 7.2, 23.5°−26.5°C (74°−80°F).

Usually only 7.5−12.5cm (3−5in) long and 2.8cm ($1\frac{1}{8}$in) thick, red brown in colour, overlaid with filigree pattern and a pale undercarriage, a long snout mouth. The male has a long thin red line, his body is wider due to the long row of skin folds in his undercarriage where the eggs are hatched.

It is the male who carries and hatches the eggs.

Spawning is done in top waters, and needs to be induced by multi-twigged areas in murky light inter-

111

spersed with mildly lit clear waters. Cleanliness is appreciated; sterilization is overdoing it.

Spawning time darkens and brings out the male colours and patterns as he swims above, ahead, around and finally alongside the female, who is enticed to deposit the eggs in his brood pouch with an intense quivering of the rear part of her body. Repeated actions until the female is spent and the male pouch is full. Part adhesive at first, the eggs lose this as they mature. Care has to be taken as eggs falling out of the male pouch seldom hatch.

At 26.5°C (80°F) they usually hatch in 36-48 hours, and are free swimming in a week. Jerky spasms mark their movements, rather than rhythmic undulations.

A welcome newcomer to the popular fish tank range.

PLATIES (also Swordtails and Mollies). One of the most loved of the live bearers; tough, pretty and adaptable they will spawn anywhere laying not eggs but giving birth direct to fully formed baby fish, anything up to several dozen at a time. Seldom does an aquarist forget the first spawning, usually totally unexpected by him, when the graceful shoal of minute babies suddenly are seen; jerky swimmers for a few hours, and then beautiful little fish. Rapidly they grow, rapidly they colour, and rapidly you learn (alas!) to cease repeating the wonderful story to your friends — because they had already heard similar and equally wondrous news from other aquarists! Nevertheless it really is a great thrill.

In the old days we had neat divisions, and separate names, for the Red Platy, the Blue, the White, the Yellow, the Gold, the Speckled, the Wagtail, the High-fin, the Tuxedo, the Berlin, and so on. We still try and keep up with the flood of beautiful new strains that line breeding has fixed, but the very genus now has got so

inter-bred as to be scientifically 'no longer valid'. Particularly has this been accentuated by cross breeding with
Swordtails and with Mollies, two other famous line
bearers, and the Swords are also no longer valid!

The main Swordtails used to be green or red; then
came a stream of variations of which the modern favourites are High-fin and Lyre-tail types and combinations.
Fantastically beautiful fish, especially the males with
their long trailing elongation of the lower part of the
tail fin, earning the name of Swordtail.

So, too, with the velvet black Molly, the speckled, the
green, the Lyre-tail, the Sail-fin, the High-fin — to name
a few.

All the live bearers can easily be sexed; the female anal
fin (near the vent) is short and round, the male one is
long and pointed being used as a gonopodium for physical fertilisation. In addition, the male tail fin is distinctly
thicker and more pointed in the lowest part; a charac-
tersistic shown in the extreme by the Swordtail.

So inter-bred, in so many waters, at so many temperatures and conditions that almost any reasonable tank will
do. The females go on to spawn more than once after
only one fertilisation, and regularly do so in a community tank. After all, the difficult part of 'hatching eggs'
has already been taken care of inside the female; the
future young being folded in two, all the heads pointed
towards the same focal spot which accordingly swells
and darkens as the heads and eyes develop, and is
known as the 'gravid spot'. When intense in colour, the
spawning is near.

Gestation varies, especially with the nervous Mollies
whose high-strung nerves demand privacy, but a spring,
summer, autumn rhythm is 'natural'. Greedy Man often
forces throughout the year spawnings every few weeks
till the wrecked and exhausted female is spent. Excessive

113

in-breeding ought to be avoided by the infusion of new stock.

Gregarious and peaceful, these fish have all long since learnt to live with anyone anywhere. Jealousy, though is still a characteristic and two males with only one female is asking for trouble; a breeding trio of one male plus two females is usual.

Not unknown, is a change of sex — almost always from female to male. At a sort of half-way stage in this transition the process has been known to slow down or stop, resulting in a particularly ill-tempered fish.

SUCKING CATFISH (*Plecostomus*). Amazon. Length 20cm (8in). Firmly established as a favourite; it works hard cleaning up the tank, minds its own business, and is quaint to look at.

The drab markings clearly show that it prefers gloom to glare; shady nooks under rock ledges, between crevices, below overhangs, all suit it best. Often such characteristics are associated with muddy waters, but such would be fatal for this fish which gives an unmistakable clue to those who will look: its huge, sucker mouth not only enables it to grip on to ledges, although it prefers not to stick upside down but to hang tail-down, but also to resist strong water currents. Hence it likes free-flowing waters rich in oxygen; aeration is particularly helpful. A second clue is the enormous appetite it has for algae; found in clear swift waters, strongly-lit. Hence this fish needs a hiding place, well sheltered from the light, during the day; emerging at dawn and dusk to work and clean and remove algae.

Its small eyes, sub-terminal snout (rather than the vast suction-type mouth) indicate a rummaging in the bottom half among nooks and crannies, rather than an open swimmer. So, too, of course do the strongly-arched back and the flat belly. Obviously a dark base would help, sand being preferred or dirt or mud.

Again such conditions, like swift waters, seldom go with great heat so that 20°–25°C (68°–77°F) is ideal; pH 7.0, DH 8–12.

All its aspects suggest flight rather than fight; and, in fact, it can accelerate away very fast for short bursts from dangers; then hanging motionless and merged in with the surroundings, hoping to remain unnoticed. A certain restlessness accompanies this ability for limited swims so that the fish tends to be a wanderer, ranging fairly extensively in its search for food. But, emphatically, it is not a scavenger, indifferent to dirt; rather, it tends to be fastidious, with a strong preference for clean green algae.

Wild specimens have been known to reach 43cm (17in) lengths, but the usual aquarium ones are 12.5–20cm (5–8in).

Other SUCKING CATFISH have long been kept in the aquarium, with the same basic preferences and characteristics as above described. The small *Ottocinclus* types, rarely growing more than 7.5cm (3in), and liked just because of that; the medium sized *Aymonieri* from Siam, and the relatively new *Myersi* from China (which can survive in really cool temperatures of only 18.5°C (65°F). Between them these types can satisfy the demands of most aquarists.

Then, too, are the droll but lovable, 'upside down' swimmers like the *Synodontis* from Africa, with their long whiskers. Of these the Congo variety, *S. Nigriventris*, has the added advantage of not growing too large, usually less than 7.5cm (3in), and of being able to withstand much higher temperatures than the others e.g. up to 26.5°C (80°F) in comfort.

115

ORDINARY CATFISH are so well known that they scarcely need enumeration, although new varieties are constantly being imported and quite a hundred different types are now available. The old, old favourites still hold their own: the Paleatus with its spots, the Aneus with its stripes, the Leopard and the similarly-marked Melanistius, the tiny Hastatus and the red-eyed Albino, to name but a few. They are a 'must' for every tank, and, unlike their cousins, the sucking catfish, are not over sensitive to dirt. Yet even they take a dim view of a tank base wholly covered with mulm.

Basically their demands are the same, though less enthusiastic vegetarians they will eat tubifex worms and meat scraps quite eagerly. Bottom dwellers, it's the bottom 2.5cm (1in) of tank conditions and temperatures that affect them most; many aquarists tend to be careless about that particular vital area. At least thirty varieties are normally available of these peaceful, gregarious hard-workers.

SCATS (*Scatophagus argus*). Length 15cm (6in). East Pacific Coast. One of those mobile fish that go anywhere, with anybody and whom you meet wherever you go. Basically they are sea-water, ocean shore, scavengers who get carried away by their enthusiastic appetites right up the deltas, creeks and estuaries into inland brackish, and even fresh waters. Extensively found along the vast Pacific coast line they are an established aquarium favourite. Newly caught, brackish water specimens need to be slowly acclimatized to fresh water — but not to acid water — and the aquarist should beware of these 'very cheap' ones. Otherwise they are resilient, peaceful although a shade greedy with an ever-empty stomach.

Many varieties are known like the Red Tiger, or the

Green, or the Yellow but the fish tend to change both colour and even markings according to mood and condition. Provided the water is not actually acid, they can survive almost anything, and will eat algae as readily as flesh foods, worms or daphnia.

The slightly uncouth mouth, the rather untidy hotchpotch of dots and flashes, is in keeping with their scavenger characteristics. Totally lacking pride or in fierceness, they will not attack, rather they are timid and will scamper off, and are, therefore, happiest in the safety of shoals. Established shoals tend to be unruly, darting hither and thither, calling to each other, restlessly searching, always on the go; exhilarating or wearying to others! Their laterally compressed bodies show an obvious preference for crevices or reed-like thickets, and their round circular bodies indicate that water depths of 30—60cm (12—24in) are better than shallows. Their changing colours show their adaptability to bright clear waters, free flowing; to heavy overgrowths, and even to mud, provided the waters flow and do not get stagnant, an important point too often overlooked.

Aeration and a salt bath will usually tone them up. The more hunch-backed the fish, the older it is. A safe hiding place is a 'must' for lonely specimens who will rush out to grab food and then tear back to safety again. DH 10—12, pH 7.4, 24°—28°C (75°—82°F) all suit them.

SPINY EELS (*Mastocembelus argus*). Siam. Length 20cm (8in). Obviously keen on burrowing into the sand base, which should not be sharp or scratchy, therefore, the long thin body, the deep protected eyes, and the subterminal mouth all indicate that. Yet, the mouth shows more: it is part aggressive, part scavenger; in fact, it has teeth. Hence the fish likes tubifex worms and is not

117

at all interested in green stuffs; in fact, it is allergic to green water.

Like its cousin the *Plecostumus*, just described, it requires the same clear, clean fast-flowing waters, dim light, nooks and crannies of rocks, twigs or tree bark. Also it prefers a soft base, mud rather than mulm where it hunts hidden or buried flesh foods, ignoring the green plants. As a scavenger to burrow into, under and through the sand — it's unbeatable.

The small mouth makes it safe to keep in a community tank. So too are the many similar spiny eels like the West African *M. loennbergi* or the Indian *M. pancalus*.

Spawning is relatively easy, provided the aquarist follows the clues shown by the heightened breeding colours; from being drab, bottom dwellers, buried by day, they suddenly change: intense colours, and frantic day movements. This total reversal clearly explains their insistent demand for strong, twiggy, long-thick-root-like tangles just below the water surface. Without these they seldom spawn readily. DH 10, pH 7.0, 24°–26.5°C (75°–80°F) also help, as does a little-distant, but yet strong, top lighting penetrating through the tangled clumps for an hour or so before the event. The adhesive eggs are hidden in the tangles, hatch in 48-72 hours; the jerky fry staying hidden at water surface become free swimming in a week or so. A sure sign of healthy growth is when the 2.5cm (1in) long fry begin visiting the tank base, finally to desert the surface tangles altogether in a month when the snout has developed. At the age of three months the total length may still be under 7.5cm (3in). Aeration helps hatching and growth, as does dim streaky light once the eggs are laid.

Catching the adults is difficult, partly because they can accelerate rapidly, and twist and turn like a Grand

Prix car racer, and partly because they can be almost invisible, completely buried in the sand with only the snout tip breaking the surface. A planting stick run carefully a couple of centimetres below sand level dislodges them. It can be done very gently because these quaint fish are responsive and tameable. If you win their confidence they will swim into, and curl into almost any tempting net or cup-like 'home' within 15cm (6in) or so of tank base; obviously playing and showing off for you.

ZEBRA (*Brachydanio rerio*). India. Length 6cm (2½in). Another firm favourite right from the very early days. Graceful torpedo body, balanced and slim, nicely finned; obviously a very fast swimmer, with great manouvreability and energy. Add the beautifully clear cut longitudinal stripes, entirely free of smudges, and a sheening body — obviously we have a fish that loves open clean bright waters, free flowing if possible, with ample room to swim and play. Its bright clear eyes and medium mouth, slightly super terminal; its general friendly appearance, lacking in pugnacity, denote its love of companionship, its ability to stay in shoals, to laugh and to frolic in mid-to-top waters.

Coming from India where temperatures fluctuate between slight frost in winter and intense heat in summer, it therefore has a wide temperature tolerance. Its barbels, together with its bubbling energy, denote a healthy appetite; its extreme mobility is also not out of place with its short, but gay life span of three years of so.

A prolific breeder, the parents eat the free-scattered eggs with relish unless prevented by a false bottom, rough pebble base with ample crevices to trap the eggs, or some other such provision. Spawning often lasts a week or more, giving 100 to 150 eggs per day; hatching in 36-48 hours at 24°C (75°F) they become free swimming in two days. Tangles of roots, or of twigs, just below water surface and strong overhead lighting are conducive to spawning. DH 8—12, pH 7.0 to 7.5, 24°—25.5° (75°—78°F) would also help. Plenty of foods are essential, flesh rather than vegetable, though both are taken. Many are the variations:

B. albolineatus (the Pearl Danio), just as hardy and just as playful.

B. nigrofasciatus (Spotted Danio), with a lovely delicate mouth; less pushing, more gentle, and smaller — only 4.5cm ($1\frac{3}{4}$in) — this Indo-Chinese dweller tends to be overshadowed by its more boisterous cousins. It prefers slightly higher temperatures of 23.5°—26.5°C (74°—80°F), and particularly appreciates cleanliness.

B. malabaricus (Giant Danio), considerably more able to 'take care of itself' and growing to 15cm (6in) or more it clearly wants large free waters and would be too much for small fish; otherwise peaceful and gregarious.

CHAPTER SEVENTEEN

USEFUL FACTS

If your heating fails don't pour in hot water and risk cracking the glass. Fill a clean tall bottle (no smell please!) e.g. a milk bottle with very hot water and stand it in the tank with its mouth protruding above water surface. The heat from the milk bottle should maintain the temperature all night, especially if you cover the whole tank with a rug.

Proportion of litres to imperial gallons
1 litre = 1,000 cubic centimetres = 1.7598 pints.
1 cubic foot = 28.31 litres.
1 pint = 0.5679 litres.
1 Imperial gallon = 4.5459 litres = 0.1605 cubic feet.
1 United States gallon = 3.785 litres = 0.1339 cubic feet.

Weights
1 kilogram = 1,000 grams = 1,000,000 milligrams = weight of one litre of water.
1 grain = 0.065 gram.
15.432 grains = 1 gram.

Medicine dip
If you plan to give a sick fish a medicine bath for a few seconds or minutes; get a suitable sized net, dip this and the fish in the solution, leaving it free to swim inside the net, and remove both after the measured time lapse.

Catching fish
Use two nets. With the smaller one chase the fish into the bigger one, which should then be pulled upwards, not forwards.

If time permits, sink the big net right into the water, well spread out, and directly under the main feeding area; tempt the fish over the net with food, and then pull net upwards.

Syphon tube
Do not buy a rubber tube that is too short or the out-coming water is sure to spill one day. Let the tubing be amply long enough to reach full down to the floor, and have enough spare to coil inside the bucket on the floor. Now you can safely concentrate your attention on the tank end of the tubing.

Rather than let water just rush out, squeeze the rubber/plastic tubing to slow and stop the water flow as you move the tank end from one collection of dirt to another, syphoning only the dirt, with the minimum of water.

Introducing new fish
Feed the others first, extra well on this one occasion; float the container with the new fish in the tank to equalise the two water temperatures, say for five or ten minutes, and then float out the newcomers in the back corner, while the others are eating at the front.

If your fish dies
Take it back in aquarium water for the dealer to do a post-mortem examination. Do not take it back dry, but freshly preserved in water. The sooner the better.

Medicines
It is often better to build up to the full dose in two or three stages, spaced a few hours apart. Each tank water

has a 'different composition' and may contain elements to cause unexpected reactions, resulting in a dose that is 'too strong'. Sensitivity and patience are most helpful.

Live daphnia
Sometimes this goes off, say on a hot day, and contains much debris or dead daphnia. Pour all into a clean jam jar. Within seconds the dead and the sediment will sink to the bottom, leaving you free to pour out the rest carefully. If too many live daphnia stay trapped in the sediment, the jar can be refilled with water, allowed to settle and the top poured off again.

Temperature
If this seems to fluctuate unduly, is your thermometer too near the top? Is it too near the heat of the electric top lighting which can warm the top few centimetres of the water?

Replacing fish
If you have had two for a long time and one dies, please think before you replace. Has the survivor grown too large for the replacement? If so, why not buy two, and lessen the chance of bullying.

Breeding
Far better, if you have time and space, than buying a breeding pair is to get a number of young adults, allow them to grow and to pair off naturally.

Peat
Cover the base of a non-toxic (important please) container with peat and leave it soaking in rainwater all the time, replacing as you use. Say 2.5cm (1in) of peat to 15cm (6in) of water. Dim light discourages algae, etc.

123

When the peat sinks it is 'mature'; it, and the saturated water, are both excellent for fish.

The stock solution should be easy to maintain as the water gets saturated before the peat. Always keep plenty in hand, well before you need it; even two months!

If in a hurry, you can heat a peat plus six parts of water solution, even boil it. But this will be ultra strong, perhaps toxic, and should be very heavily diluted before use.

When in doubt
Part change the water with new water of the same temperature; clean the filter, including the carbon; skim the water surface; increase aeration; and feed with live foods. Dim light may help.

CHAPTER EIGHTEEN

COLDWATER AQUARIUM FISH

These are very very different from coldwater pond fish, which will be dealt with in the next chapter, and many tragic deaths arise from confusing the two. After all, you wouldn't confuse a Pekinese dog and an elephant; one can live happily in a small flat, the other can't — no matter how small the elephant or how big the flat; the basic conditions are wrong.

Most stubborn is the insensitive 'brute' of a customer, who has kept a goldfish in a bowl (or small tank) for six months or two years and refuses to recognise his cruelty — because that is the word — cruelty. A human will live locked up in a dungeon for years — tyrants of old proved it; similarly will a fast-moving, quick-growing, rapidly-oxygen-consuming goldfish 'live' in the cramped frustration of an indoor tank, stunted in growth and suffering in slow suffocation, as it ekes out its oxygen. In a pond the goldfish could flourish for a quarter of a century and be 46cm (18in) long.

Many lovely fish are available for the indoor aquarium, including gold coloured ones. But, these indoor fish have short rounded bodies, they do not grow so large or need so much oxygen or so much swimming space; and they are happy in a balanced tank. Because the water in a proper coldwater tank need never be changed, the principles for balance are exactly the same as discussed earlier.

ORANDA is now a great favourite, and comes over in quantities from China, via Hong Kong, so that its once prohibitive price has dissolved into mere fractions. Often gold coloured, sometimes in combinations of reds, whites or even yellows, it grows a fascinating 'lion's mane' round its head from the age of thirty months or so. A huge 'mane' or cape right over the top of the head, raised well up, and pimpled like a raspberry; most distinctive! Its temperature tolerance is wide, though it no more likes freezing than we do and now expects the raised standards of a house warmed to 15.5°C (60°F) or more; ideally would settle for 20°–23°C (68°–73°F); for old water; acid say of pH 6.8 but soft, say of DH 2–6. Yet it will not grumble over much at London water, which is much harder, and will settle down to most foods and temperatures. The bodies of the best specimens are of even roundness, in the curved back as well as the full tummy, nicely filled flanks; a smoothly-curving dorsal fin on the back half the body width, an evenly-matched flowing caudal (or tail) fin half the body length, and two nicely-pointed downwards pectoral (or breast) fins. When matured, its lion's mane should fully cover its head right down to the eyes, and the face should be spheroid, not pointed. But that's an ideal; it's very very rare — after all, you wouldn't expect all women to have the alluring beauty of Helen of Troy. If you have such a specimen you can ask by comparison the same high price as a slave trader of old might have asked for Helen. Alternatively, you can just settle for one nine-months old, colour gold, docile and affectionate.

Breeding the Oranda is normal. Temperature and water as already described; peat in the filter; toned-up by feeding on sterilised live foods of tubifex, daphnia, mashed earth-worms, chopped up white worms, a good flake food; two specimens of 3 or 4 years of age can be

introduced in the evening to a prepared tank at least
90cm × 30cm × 30cm (36in × 12in × 12in). Either the
tank will be sterilised by an ozoniser; or by hand-boiling
the gravel, scouring the tank in clean hot water, and
rinsing all plants, rocks, etc., in one of the latest aquarium
preparations for anti-septic use; please, please note that

Fig. 12 Veiltail Oranda

Fig. 13 Comet-tail Oranda

the antiseptic is not a normal household one, but a special aquarium preparation.

By mid-afternoon next day the spawning chase should have begun, with the male driving and nuzzling the flanks of the female, and resulting in large numbers of eggs caught by the soft spawning plants like Myriophyllum. There is no real need to use more than one properly-conditioned male for the driving-chase, as he should be fully able to produce enough milt to fertilise all the eggs. After spawning, both parents should be removed.

One thousand fry may well hatch in 3—4 days at 24°C (75°F), and will demand frequent and heavy feeding with infusoria (which you can now buy ready prepared), with very finely-powdered egg yolk, with newly hatched brine shrimps, micro worms, and finally with powdered dried foods and sifted daphnia in about two weeks. These foods are now so readily available from the specialist dealer that there is little need to describe the detailed techniques for home production.

Many factors govern the success of the spawning. Water has to be right; if your fish delay courtship, then have a good look at pH, DH, temperature, temporary hardness of CH or 'buffered solids', and so on. If you seem to have too many of the diseased white-opaque eggs don't despair (because the other healthy and transparent ones are difficult to see) but add a special aquarium antiseptic, dim or darken the light in and round the tank, change the filter material including plenty of activated charcoal, use an ozoniser. If the fry are slow of growth change the food (was it too big or too small), raise or lower the temperature 1°C (2°F), raise or lower the water level 2.5cm (1in) per 3 days, part-change the water with prepared water of as near the same as possible to that now discarded, increase or decrease the intensity and duration of the top-lighting, and better still alter its colour or angle of penetration.

Of course, you will be looking out for water enemies like Hydra, which latch onto fry or even to adult fish and are tenacious parasites that can kill unless forced off; you know that too much shade is not better than too little; that all tools, and foods, need to be sterilised; that fry hate, positively hate, draughts and like warm moist air, trapped by a top cover just above water level; that the water surface should be clean and scum free — how would you like oil on your gill plates? These gill plates are sensitive even in an adult fish. Constipation is not unknown in short, rounded bodies, so green stuffs and laxative daphnia are appreciated.

Once hatched, a fortnight old and eating dried foods, your fry now want room — plenty of room. How healthy do you think human children would be if they were kept packed in a room with no outlet, and for years at a time?

The urge for living space encourages breeders to cull the fry at an early age, selecting the better specimens and discarding the rest. The caudal (tail) fin should be large and evenly divided into two with the split showing along the top; placing the fry in a white bowl enables this to be seen.

Uneven growth of the fry means things are not going well. The hints just given should be re-examined, and in case of doubt part-change the water lest invisible fish urine, etc., be too prominent. Meticulous care to equalise the temperatures of the two waters must be remembered. The roots of floating plants like Duckweed take waste matter from the water, the leaves give shade, and oxygen is trapped in the water; all good points. Yet scum can also get trapped in the leaves and do great harm; removing it is tedious, as the whole plant has to be scooped-out and rinsed in running water and the

129

tank surface skimmed before replacing the plants.

The rate of growth depends on general conditions, notably on foods, temperature, state of the water and on the amount of room. The better the conditions the quicker they grow and the sooner they change colour. Of course, you certainly would not 'force breed' your fish — see page 74 — and a target of nine months for body sizes of 4cm ($1\frac{1}{2}$in) would be reasonable. At optimum temperatures of 20°−23°C (68°−73°F) fish will eat four times a day, above and below that they get increasingly sluggish. If your fish keep too much to the top waters only, leaving the rest of the tank empty, then all is not well. Temperature too low, or water not sweet are the usual culprits; uneaten foods need to be syphoned-off, and at four feedings a day, this may frequently be advisable. Variety in the foods cannot be overstressed. Water deeper than 15−23cm (6−9in) may even be proving a little too deep for the fry; it is not usual to alter the level more than 2.5cm (1in) at a time, spaced 3−7 days apart.

However, Orandas are fairly easy to breed and the stress above on possible problems is only the better to guide the customer isolated from a specialist dealer. The same breeding techniques apply to the other coldwater aquarium fish now described.

The LIONHEAD is very similar to the Oranda except that it has no dorsal (back) fin and its caudal (tail) fin is far shorter. By contrast, however, its 'lion's mane' growth is enormous — quite incredible. Again showing only after 24−36 months. As expected with such growth it has some difficulty in breathing and is peculiarly susceptible to impure water, ideally preferring oxygen rich, crystal clear, slightly moving waters, old but acid, pH 6−8, soft of DH 2−6, and warmed to 20.5°−23.5°C (69°−74°F). Likes aeration, and often is seen to tickle its lion's mane growth in a stream of air bubbles. Otherwise hardy, but for a tendency to constipation. Of course, the Oranda has the same strengths and weaknesses, but not to such a noticeable degree.

The body of the Lionhead, only in the ideal, should also be nicely rounded and plump, and should be free of humps, of indentations, or of elongation particularly on the back and at the caudal peduncle, i.e. where the body joins the tail. Its colours are of the same as the Oranda, usually gold, often red, with or without combinations of white and of yellow. But new strains keep coming along, like the amusing 'red-cap' marking on the forehead.

Fig 14 Lionhead

Once fabulously expensive, it is now available from time to time at popular prices.

The CELESTIAL is really the quaintest of fish. Some slight traces of the lion's mane of the Oranda remain as a mere hint, completely overshadowed by two enormous telescopic eyes pointing straight upwards, not forwards. The bulbous protrusions of the eyes seem to make a sort of hollow valley between, on a slightly-flattened plateau of a head.

The rest of the body is rounded and plump in the ideal, but with a tendency to elongation in practice; no dorsal fin on the smooth line of the back; with a marked caudal peduncle or 'bridge' on to which joins a magnificent tail, very reminiscent of that of the Oranda and similarly divided. Unfortunately only too prevalent is a disturbed line on the back, some hump or indentation, where the dorsal fin would have been. A really superb pair would fetch the price of a motor car, so please don't be too pernickety for the relatively modest price you are likely to be asked.

Colouring and ideal conditions as for the Lionhead. Feeding is obviously only from above, and floating scum on the water surface would be disastrous as those vulnerable short-sighted eyes peered into the oily film.

The BUBBLE EYE is like a debauched celestial, having two great big pouches under each eye; the whole eye looks as though it's dropped — if ever you've seen a saint with a halo that's slipped you'll know what a bubble eye looks like. The larger the bubble the more expensive the fish.

Continuing on the downward path we land up with a PEARL SCALE. The puffiness has now descended to the body so that the scales have a marked tendency to stand out. Prominent and separative, not at all aligned and at oneness. The head is still flattened but the mouth area resembles more a pig's snout; the pimpled lion's mane is absent, and the eyes are featured rather than prominent. They anxiously focus forward following the line of the snout and the search for food. The dorsal fin is seldom evenly curved, the caudal peduncle, or bridge to the tail, looks as though its lower part has been distorted by being squeezed flat. The tail fin varies; it can be like that of an Oranda, of a Lionhead, or of a Fantail. Yet, you will like its droll appearance, its hardy uncomplaining attitude to life; its mixture of colours, often white sometimes just the first colour you happened to have thought of, with red, gold, black in descending order of frequency.

Both the Bubble Eye and the Pearl Scales are becoming established in increasing numbers. Their ideal conditions and breeding habits are as those of the Oranda. As with the Celestials, the fry do not show their breed characteristics for a long time.

The TELESCOPIC-EYED BLACK MOOR is still an old old favourite though now being challenged by the above newcomers. Two forward-pointing but short-sighted protruding telescopic eyes, a lovely rounded and plump body of an Oranda, with a superb high-peaked curved back dorsal fin, a neat caudal peduncle joining a lovely tail more luxuriant than that of the Oranda, unless it's a veil-tailed telescopic-eyed Black Moor with a beautiful flow of finnage worthy of that name.

Fig. 15 Chinese Moor

133

The body colour is pitch velvet-smooth black, with a glorious bloom of blackness as smooth as a ripe peach.

Such superb specimens would again be the price of a motor-car; sold in quantities they are still lovely, although bronze and bronze-sheening may intrude on the pitch black. Having been 'line-bred' for so long its body shape is consistently of a good standard if slightly more oval than round.

Hardy, but dislikes the cold and wilts at temperatures below 14°C (57°F), otherwise responds and breeds like the Oranda. Slow moving as you would expect with those eyes it can be hand fed; as indeed can all the fish just described. Naturally, the age-old rule applies of feeding in the same place, at the same time, with the same mannerisms (the way you lift or bang the cover, shake/thump/display the food tin, etc.) so that the slow and the shy fish can get into position and are not displaced by the swift and the thrusting.

The eyes being so attractive, or repellent — which still makes them distinctive and so desirable — has led to many strains being bred with telescopic eyes. The telescopic-eyed calico fantail, with gay colours of a Shubunkin and the rounded body of the Oranda; the more prized telescopic-eyed Veiltail, and the even more rare telescopic-eyed Veiltail Calico.

VEILTAIL. Still the most prized and still the most difficult to get. Those who really have good Veiltails simply don't like parting with them and only very inferior ones tend to be occasionally offered for general sale. The main trouble is that the strain has not really been fixed; from superb parents the progeny are mostly ordinary. However, we all keep trying and sooner or later success will come.

The ideal body of a Veiltail is round, with no trace of

Fig. 16 Veiltail

oval, really full flanks; even the head and 'face' are round without snoutiness. The magnificently flowing tail (or caudal) fin is quite twice the length of the body, often more, the fork is entirely absent, and the veils fall gracefully all the way down.

The colours can be anything, as people try breeding all manner of cross fertilisations to fix the developed tail. Gold is the favourite, of course, also red, blue, white, yellow, and combinations thereof. Very popular, too, are the mottled colours of the Shubunkin type, i.e. the body scales are transparent and the colours below show through as blues, greens, blacks, reds, golds and other streaks and blotches, with some overriding sheen, with blue rated highest.

Dragging all that finnage around makes the fish slow and liable to fatigue; hence it is an easy prey to disease and to rougher companions. Fin rot and constipation are particularly to be guarded against, and its nerves should not be jangled too much when it tires — it simply must have places for rest and privacy, in fact it normally expects to have the whole tank to itself and its mate,

135

with you waiting on it hand and foot as befits its status. Naturally, you must do everything just right — the tank must be warm, 23°—24.5°C (73°—76°F); clean, waters of pH 6—8 and of DH 3—6; well-lit, to encourage plant life, as it likes greenstuffs in its diet, and adequate shade; the finesse of aeration is to be expected, as is your regular traipse to the specialist dealer to buy live foods. But you, the slave, will adore the Veiltail; it really is most most beautiful, and it will twiddle you round its little fin.

Fig. 17 Fantail

Breeding is a real challenge, not so much for getting a spawning, as for rearing a good fry. The golden rules are well-established — basically to work with Mother Nature and her deep rhythms; for example, spring and summer spawnings are best, autumn ones are good, but winter ones tend to produce weaker fry, however efficient are the artificial conditions provided by the breeder.

Plenty of space by culling out the poorer specimens early, really early, is a kindness to the others. Also of help is a slight increase in warmth — say 0.5°—1°C (1°—2°F) but no more or the growth may be 'forced' and this will permanently weaken the fish, extra aeration, live foods as soon as the young can take them, one centimetre extra water-depth per week, and, of course, cleanliness. The latter can be aided by very mild disin-

fectants as sold in the specialists shops, or even by
adding methylene blue — enough to colour the water
the lightest shade of blue.

One very good tip, not too well-known, is that if the
spawnings are too prone to disease, keep the newly-laid
eggs and the just-hatched fry in ultra-dim light (even in
total darkness) for the first twenty-four to thirty-six
hours. It may inhibit the growth of the fry a little, but
hinders parasites and diseases even more.

FANTAIL. Still with us, of course, still popular, peaceful, hardy, colourful, braving impossible conditions
with a smile, as its very cheapness encourages some
people to dump it into any old tank in any old condition. The body is often more oval than the ideal of
rounded; its dorsal fin is less peaked, less graciously
curved, and starts further back from the head than is the
case with an Oranda; and so too with its slightly stumpy
tail and breast fins. Frequent mixed breeding has produced reds, golds, whites, blacks, yellows, greens and
any combinations you want; reds and golds are still the
most popular. As already stated it will live anywhere and
eat anything; given a chance it would like the same conditions as the Oranda. Web-tails, tri-tails, spade-tails,
and single tails are all well known, as are the calico mixture
of body colours normally found in the Shubunkin.
Telescopic eyes are also obtainable, of course. The Fantail
is basically an aquarium fish which can be kept in a pond,
and be expected to survive a winter and the rough-and-
tumble of the wild out-doors. The Shubunkin is basically
a pond fish, adapted in days of old to life in the sheltered,
but restricted, aquarium as in those days the other fish
described in this chapter were not widely available. We,
however, now propose to put the Shubunkin back in the
pond, and to talk of it in the next chapter.

CHAPTER NINETEEN

POND FISH

As already stressed at the beginning of the last chapter, pond fish are quite, quite distinct from those of the cold-water aquarium; in the pond, fish grow large, 46cm (18in) or more in length, live for 25 or 40 years even, and need lots of space in length, width and height, with an abundance of insect and bacteria life, not really possible indoors.

Since the days when Europe and America were forest-ridden wildernesses inhabited by nomads, and the Chinese Emperors ruled in ancient Cathay, the GOLDFISH have held firmly to their position as favourites in the outdoor pond. It's quite a record. But they are marvellous fish; colourful, happy, gregarious, peaceful, hardy, uncomplaining; tolerating any foods, waters or temperatures; breeding easily; they have all the virtues. Famous throughout the planet, everyone seems to love Goldfish, and as pets they are longer established than horses or dogs. The ancient Incas of South America had no horses — but had Goldfish; the great monastries of bygone Egypt of the earliest Pharoahs were guarded not by dogs or horses but by cats — they too had Goldfish. In all probability so does your child, right now, have or want a Goldfish, as you yourself probably did years ago.

Goldfish (scientific name is *Carassius auratus*) come in many colours. Usually born dark, almost black, they range up through black, bronze, white red, yellow and gold; occasionally going through the whole range and reaching perfection in a lovely gold colour in two to five years, sometimes getting permanently stuck somewhere along the line and almost invariably with a mixture of colours. The time taken to change colour depends on general conditions, notably the quality of the parents, the condition of the water, the foods and space available, and the temperature. The general guidance of chapter 14 very much applies to pond fish.

The temperature tolerance of Goldfish is truly astonishing; frozen and literally imprisoned in solid blocks of ice as the pond freezes, and yet these fish have been known to survive; at the distant end of the temperature scale they live in Equatorial Africa, when men wilt and die of sunstroke. Please, however, be kind; these hardy fish don't enjoy ill-treatment; temperature fluctuations have to be extremely gradual to cover wide differences; and most of the fish likely to be sold in Europe or America would prefer 10°–20°C (50°–68°F). Similarly, with water, their endurance is great from almost pure acid of pH 6.2 to almost pure alkaline of pH 7.8, they would choose pH 6.8 to pH 7.2; and in hardness from DH 4 to DH 12, with an optimum of DH 4–8.

So much cross-breeding has gone on in the last two decades that distinctions between all fish are shaded rather than clear-cut. This applies generally to tropical, to coldwater aquarium and to coldwater pond fish, including the Goldfish; so that all the separative names of the fish mentioned in my books have that reservation of shading one into the other. Yet Goldfish can be said to live twenty-five years and to grow to 40–50cm (16–20in) in length under ideal conditions.

Breeding is best done in large volumes of water, which in practice, means a pond. Mother Nature usually provides sufficient stimulus in England for four spawnings per year; late spring, say April–May; twice in midsummer, say June and August; and once in early autumn, say September; but, of course, conditions vary and therefore so do times and frequency. Water conditions, supply of natural live foods, and temperatures are very important. Like so many natural beings, Goldfish seem psychically to know when warm weather is coming and they start their spawning chases, with the males driving the females, right at the beginning of a fine spell. 'Flock' spawning is still the most popular, i.e. a number of males driving a number of females, jointly laying and fertilising the scattered eggs; but a well-conditioned single male usually provides enough milt to fertilise the eggs of a female if carefully selective breeding is desired, in which case the pair are better mated in specially separated water, and the eggs rigorously isolated and hatched under controlled conditions.

Flock spawning in a pond produces the hardiest specimens as only the strong tend to survive; yet the most prized specimens because of colour, shape, finnage, etc., are obviously better hand-selected and protected in the controlled conditions of separated waters, and where they won't be swamped by their wilder companions or by sudden changes of conditions and of temperatures. Furthermore, in a natural pond the moment of spawning is frequently precipated by the whims of a weather change; in controlled waters the spawning pair are usually separately conditioned-up and put together only at the optimum time, with extraneous creatures and influences kept in check. Unlike the live-bearing tropical fish where one single fertilisation by a male will enable the female to go on and independently spawn several lots of baby fish, separated over months, the female Goldfish comes to each mating completely free of the influences of previous spawnings; her eggs are fertilised only after being laid and can be fertilised solely by the male then present, and the resulting fry can be guaranteed to have only those particular parents — a great help in selective breeding.

Incidentally, sexing the fish is not quite as automatic as people think, and many a 'breeding pair' turn out to be nothing of the sort. The theory is that the male shows white raised dots on his gill plates, and the female is fatter, especially on her left side when looked at from above and behind. The white spots are the terminals of the tubes through which the male ejects his fertilising milt, and are visible normally only at spawning condition and readiness. Sometimes, even then the terminals do not protrude enough to be visible. Conversely, the female may show distinct white flecks and spots, including on her gill plates, and, although these are not developed terminals, a mistake in sex identification is easy. Similarly, both the male and the female have to be of the same type for the fullness of the female to be apparent; in these days of cross fertilisation many a plump male has been taken for the female when compared with a leaner female of a different (and leaner) strain. By far the best is a natural pair that have been known to have previously spawned together.

Bearing the above points in mind let us now attempt a spawning in the pond. The rigours of the winter being over, comes the testing time of early spring when fish emerge from hibernation in fits and starts as the weather literally blows hot and cold, and disease and death are in evidence. It was the strain of the winter just passed that harmed the fish, although the physical results did not manifest till the fish emerged from their torpor as the weather warmed. Having restored the fish and pond to health, as per the instructions in the next chapter, we start toning-up the fish to breeding condition with live foods like chopped garden worm, red tubifex worms,

141

live daphnia and so on. We take our cue for feeding from the fish themselves — when they are seen to start searching actively for food, to try and suck algae off the pond sides, then the time has come.

The earlier the spawning the better, as the fry have a chance to grow bigger and stronger before having to face the next winter; if several warm spells of weather have slipped by without activity and March has passed into April, then the pond conditions are clearly not right. Chapter 14 should give help in finding the cause.

Finally, spawning takes place, and we would do well to keep an eye on the pond temperature; 15.5°–18.5°C (60°–65°F) is usually more productive than the ranges above or below, although the eggs and the fry should have their temperature raised and kept at 21°–23.5°C (70°–74°) if they are being transferred to separated water, warmed by the sun or by artifical means. Hatching is fairly quick, some 4 or 5 days as a rule; a delay of ten days means a low temperature of 15.5°C (60°F) or poor water.

If the eggs and, therefore, the fry have been left in the original pond there is not much more to be done but to hope and to watch them grow. The importance of really thick clumps of plants, and of general hiding places, has already been stressed because all fish, including the parents, will try and eat them. So prolific are the numbers, however, that a few are more or less certain to survive.

If the eggs have been brought into separated waters, then a temperature raised over twelve hours and afterwards maintained at 21°–23.5°C (70°–74°F) will hasten the hatching to about four days; temperatures at 26.5°C (80°F) would hasten the process more but would weaken the fry. The eyes of the fry become visible after 48-60 hours, and the alevin can be seen moving inside

142

the egg a day or so later. Gentle disinfectant, of the aquarium type only please, can help to keep down the number of infertile white-opaque eggs, provided, and always provided, that the water is sweet, clean and of the pH and DH already suggested. Aeration may well be useful.

On hatching, the fry make their first dash for freedom, and dart away to find some sheltering plant or rock where they hang motionless. Now is the danger point, as the fry are vulnerable to anything from draughts, temperature changes, altering pH or DH, and all enemies including even small water boatmen, water beetles and dragonflies. Sometimes the eggs of these get caught up in the fish eggs; one reason for raising the hatching temperature to 21°–23.5°C (70°–74°F) was to mature the fish eggs quickly so as to help save them from these enemies because some like the larvae of gnats and midges eat the eggs as well.

Frequent feeding with infusoria brings on the fry rapidly once they have absorbed the yolk sac of food they are born with, and begin moving about. Infusoria can today be bought readily prepared, as can be the increasingly larger and more solid foods needed at each stage of growth. A very good precaution is to move the best of the fry, as soon as they really start swimming, to a different container so that water enemies or their eggs are left behind; of course the fry have to be individually hand-picked and moved, say with the aid of a white-lined saucepan. For example, the eggs of a newt hatch in about the same time as those of the Goldfish, and a week-old newt would decimate a spawn of fry. Fortunately this can be detected by its lighter colour and tendency to sit at the bottom. Obviously the new water will be the same as the old, including depth which can later be increased by a couple of centimetres per week from its original 15—23cm (6—9in). Care should be taken, not to introduce more enemies with plants, live foods, etc., all introductions being carefully screened and sterilised. Frequent feedings can foul the water, which may have to be part changed; overcrowding is fatal, just fatal.

Within two weeks the fry should have moved off infusoria, and finely powdered yolks of eggs, to micro worms, brine shrimp eggs and foods like small powdered foods and flakes, oatmeal, frozen tubifex and so on till by the age of three months they should be eating normally. Body development and colouring are now concentrated upon, and space being at a premium the best specimens must be kept in roomy waters; the others could now be put back in the original pond. The better fish may show colour changes from 4 to 8 months, although it may be 24 months before some of the others change. If the fish now survive the coming winter, their first, they are through the worst and will soon be thinking about breeding in their turn. The cycle is complete.

Fig. 18 Comet

The COMET is one of the many fine examples derived from the Goldfish, which it resembles strongly in body and in colouring, but has a lovely large forked tail-fin.

144

Fast-swimming, its body is slightly elongated and its fins more pointed, all giving the impression of grace with speed, strengthened by the great north-to-south arc of a tail fin streaking backwards almost three-quarters of the body length. Originally found only in the hard-scaled Goldfish types it now can have the transparent scales of a Shubunkin, and can even have telescopic eyes — a strange contraction of a body built for speed with short-sighted vulnerable eyes.

The normal Comets, however, have eyes of a particular clarity so that they see above as well as along and below; naturally, therefore, they tend to be top swimmers which makes them clearly visible in a pond. Peaceful and hardy, they have the living and breeding characteristics of a Goldfish, and are best pleased in shoals being friendly creatures.

The GOLDEN ORFE (*Idus idus*) and its original but now neglected cousin, the Silver Orfe, are also top swimmers that look their best in a shoal. Like the Comet and most top swimmers they have no barbels and their tummy is lighter in colour than their back; the stream-lined body, forward-pointing mouth, and clear 'all-round' eyes are obviously designed for speed. As you would expect with such a body they like clear, clean

Fig. 19 Orfe

open waters, well-lit and teeming with live foods which they will chase vigorously, even to eating small insects from the air who venture too near the water surface.

145

But they need oxygen for all that energy, and wilt as soon as the water content of oxygen decreases, either because the water gets foul or because it gets too hot. Given oxygen they will stand almost any water, food, conditions, or temperature; they hate a foul-smelling pond, small and crowded, on a sultry oppressive afternoon just before a thunderstorm, and would greatly appreciate a hosepipe playing in clean cool water — especially if this fell in a gentle arc from a watering-rose held or tied several feet above pond level.

The top colouring is a soft golden yellow with a silver yellow tummy; its fins are often flecked or tinged and can include a touch of redness. Black marks along the curve of the back are not unknown. Given room and oxygen these lovely Golden Orfe will live for some 30 years and grow to a full 45cm (18in), retaining their slimness to the end.

Their breeding and general habits are as described for the Goldfish. To show their adaptability, one breeder listed the foods he had given them; 'Bemax', rolled oats, packet foods, normal dried foods, all kinds of live food (which are naturally preferred) like the chopped-up garden worm, white worms, daphnia, mosquito larva, tubifex worms, freshwater shrimps, water louse, maggots, various shell-backed crustaceans, e.g. snails, mussels, most insects including blue-bottles, houseflies and wasps; also strips of meat, chopped horse heart or liver, the entrails of a chicken, etc. Yet they are peaceful and gregarious and utterly suitable for a clean pond.

Scardinius erythrophthalmus, the GOLDEN RUDD (and the Silver Rudd) is another popular top swimmer, barbel-free with a tummy lighter in colour than its back, but it is not so extreme or so vigorous as the Orfe and is more likely to cruise slowly in top to middle waters, rather

Fig. 20 Rudd

than near the surface only. The back is bronze-brown
with a sheen like a 'brass undercoating' showing through
the brown; its flanks also have an 'undercoat' of sheen
but more green than brass in colour; the tummy is
silvery sheen. The outer margins of the fin are a nice
clear red, as is its striking eye, and sometimes the mouth
too. In really good specimens the brown-brass sheen of
the back gets a tonal lift and changes into a red-brass
sheen which also tips the back and tail fins especially.
It grows to 30cm (12in) and can live for 10 years or so.
Its breeding and general habits are similar to those of
the Goldfish.

Leaving the leaner, faster top-swimmers we come on
to the mid-winter dwellers who tend to be a little more
comfortably built and tranquil.

The SHUBUNKIN seems the best known and the most
popular. Its scales are not hard and opaque, as is normal,
but are soft and quite transparent so that the body
colours show through; this characteristic led to the myth
that the Shubunkin was not hardy and could not stand
the rough-and-tumble of the pond, a myth long since
exploded by living proof to the contrary. As the reader
knows, all fish have a protective covering of soft slimy
mucus to inhibit the lodgement of foreign organisms.
Blue is the most prized underlying sheen, mottled with a
super-imposed mosaic of streaks, spots and blotches in

147

which jostle together reds, golds, blacks, violets, greens and yellows. Lovely it looks too, and the great pity is that much of this subtle beauty is lost when viewed

Fig. 21 Higoi Carp

from above. In a tank, and looked at from eye level the flanks are gloriously coloured in an angled, reflected light; this was one of the temptations for putting the Shubunkin in an aquarium. Its friendly, easy-going tolerance makes it as much at home there as in a pond; given a choice it would prefer a nice large clean and balanced pond — as it really is hardy and not susceptible to reasonable temperature variations. Inter-breeding has produced tremendous variations, including veiltail, fantail, fork tail, even telescopic eyes, but the purists still hold to two main types: the Bristol and the London — the Bristol being more of the elongated body and high finnage of a Comet, and the London being more full and shorter-finned as for the Goldfish. Both types prefer blue as the predominating colour, and all respond to the same general conditions and care as for the Goldfish.

Fig. 22 Mirror Carp

148

HIGOI (*Cyprinus carpio*) are a sort of improved Shubunkin developed largely by the Japanese copying the Chinese, as has happened with other fish before. The variations, including the Koie types now being marketed, are amazing and many are most striking. The lovely colours and patterns of the Shubunkin are reproduced in multifold patterns added to which are droll barbels, squat body shapes alternating with the conventional, telescopic eyes, and all kinds of finnage in addition. Most grow large, 45cm (18in) or more being possible, and live for very many years — forty being not unknown. Hardy, again obeying the general conditions as for the Goldfish, with the exception that the Japanese and USA imports have a preference for soft acid waters of pH 6.8, DH 4—6, and for temperatures of 18.5°–21°C (65°–70°F). Slow moving, they tame very easily and will readily eat from your hand; placid, to a marked degree, it would take a lot to shake their nerves, they are, unfortunately, sitting targets for water enemies.

Fig. 23 Tench

All ponds need some bottom feeders to grub along the mulm and silt and help keep the water from going foul. Not really recommended is the ubiquitous catfish which everyone knows, because it grows very large indeed and can most certainly nip the fins of the more decorative fish. Unusual this fin-nipping, because most of the tropical catfish are peaceful. A recommended alternative is the GREEN TENCH (*Tinea tinea*), which is peaceful as well as industrious. The drab dark green makes them inconspicuous, almost invisible, although they do come to top waters to sunbathe from time to time especially in the early sunshine after a cold spell. Conventional 'goldfishy' body except that the back has the characteristic arc of a bottom-feeder. The Golden Tench has a more bronze-gold than a green-bronze suggestion of a sheen and is sometimes preferred for its lighter colour. Yet the main job of both is at the pond base. Both, too, have a particularly thick covering of body mucus — they would need it to grub around the base — on to which other fish can be seen trying to rub-off irritating foreign parasites and organisms. Hence the name of doctor fish for these patient and docile tench.

Of course Mother Nature helped by Man produced other types of pond fish like the Bitterling that never grows above 8cm (3in); or the basically river fish accustomed to moving waters that can be forced into a still pond, i.e. the Gudgeon (a good scavenger), the Minnow (best in a shoal), the Bleak (again miniature), and so on. But these are not recommended. Nor too are the pugnacious Sunfish, Bass, Pike, and other carnivorous hunters.

CHAPTER TWENTY

THE POND

Several important decisions need to be made first, before taking any action; made correctly, the pond will give great pleasure, made wrongly and very easily you can end up with a green, slimy, smelly mess.

Is the pond to be concrete, plastic or plastic-lined?

Where is it to be placed? Is the spot cold, is it sunny, are the trees overhanging, is it on high ground? The answers to those questions help determine the success or failure for years to come.

When installing the pre-fabricated plastic pond it is advisable to dig the soil up rather more than you will eventually need, so as to make absolutely sure that the pond is even. Any variation from the true, for example as the pond weight beds down, the soil which has been moistened and made pliable by subsequent rain, will show very clearly in the sloping water-line. In fact the water-line will seem to exaggerate the slope. The excavated earth is usually piled outside the shallow edge of the pond which should be towards the sunniest spot; the piled-up excavated earth should slope from the north side down (southwards) to shallow water, to give a maximum sun-trap for plants and fish; some bricks in the form of a protective wall will inhibit excess soil from washing into the pond.

Unless a plastic pond is really deep enough it will always tend to give trouble in English climates; by 'deep enough' is meant at least one metre (3ft). That is the big

151

headache. Many lovely shapes, designs and colours are widely and cheaply available in pre-fabricated plastic ponds, easy to install, light to transport; a great temptation to buy but extremely difficult to maintain clean and balanced if unprotected from frost and sun. Within the normal lifetime of a pond the English climate is practically certain to freeze water to a depth of 1 metre (3ft), and relatively frequent freezings to 30—60cm (12—24in) are likely; in addition, the same variable climate is certain to heat-up too much the first 90cm (36in) depth of water at some time in the pond's life, and is likely to overheat the first 30—60 cm (12—24in) frequently. Neither the heat nor the cold help fish-happiness, nor, too, does the suddenness with which the weather is likely to switch from hot to cold, a change which is felt by the fish more quickly in shallow water, who get weakened if this happens often — as it is almost certain to do. Relatively deep water cools or heats far more slowly and allows fish time to get adjusted. There is no need for the whole pond to be over one metre deep; shallows and varying heights reducing to only 15cm (6in) are desirable, even essential for the fish to be able to spawn their eggs.

A compromise is to dig a hole of the required dimensions and line it with plastic, waterproof sheetings obtainable in various colours. These come ready-tailored to popular sizes and are complete with trimmers to face the edge of the pond, partly to hold the sheetings firmly in place and partly to enhance the edges. Met with the usual howl of protest that greets most innovations, these sheetings do serve a useful purpose. A useful guide in ordering sheetings for a previously-dug hole is length of the hole twice the depth, for one side; and the width plus twice the depth for the other measurement. For example, a hole 90cm × 120cm × 45cm (36in ×

48in × 18in) deep would need a sheet 3m × 2m (9ft × 7ft).

The danger is, of course, that the sheetings get punctured. Punctures can be quickly enough mended once all the trouble of finding them and emptying the pond has been gone through, but in fairness, this should not happen too easily if you have bought sheetings of sufficient thickness, adequately-lined the corners and contours so that no one part of the sheeting gets over-stretched and strained, and have kept the total depth to about 1.8m (6ft) or less so that the weight and pressure of the water are reasonable. It does help considerably to remove all abrasive stones, including those buried 8cm (3in) below the top soil and which might well work their way up to contact with the sheeting, and to place several layers of newspaper as a lining between the soil and the sheeting. Sedge peat, fine sand, sawdust, and sifted soil — used individually or mixed — make an excellent protective lining for the plastic sheeting. Newspapers can still be useful, especially up the sloping sides. All air pockets must, of course, be smoothed right-out, particularly on the sloping edges which have a tendency to cave-in, as do artifical contours, unless underpinned and supported.

Size need not be a problem. Many a local authority has now followed the pioneering example of Hereford-shire who constructed a huge artificial pond on a ten-acre site using sheeting. The complex included a stream, cascading over shallow rapids, shaped ponds heavily planted, outlets into a big lake — and this in spite of porous soil. The sheeting alone was enough: of heavy tensile strength, laid in large square pieces half the area of a tennis court, they were put directly onto the soil, except for the protection of newspaper lining, and were cold-sealed by joining with 10cm wide tapes.

So, it can be done with sheeting, yet for sheer durability the concrete pond is hard to beat. It can be made
to any shape, depth, or size and seems to last forever.
The all-important question of where to site it will be
discussed presently; for the moment let us look at its
construction. First, it must withstand frost, severe
frost, year after year; the concrete at the base of a
3m X 60cm X 60cm (10ft X 2ft X 2ft) pond would
need to be an effective 30cm (12in) thick at the base
and a genuine 12cm (5in) thich at the top as it tapers-up.
The more outward sloping the vertical sides, the more
easily can winter ice lift up and the less the strain on the
concrete. It is surprising how great an easement a slope
of 5° off-vertical can make. The corners and any vulnerable curves need to be reinforced. Skimping will just
not pay in the long run.

Next, the shape. The exterior can be absolutely anything you like: square, rectangualar, with curved ends,
kidney-shaped, lotus-shaped, circular; a single unit or a
combination of two or more separated waters linked by
channels that wind and curve, go straight or criss-cross,
are wide and deep and/or narrow and shallow — the
separated waters being at one level or many, with water
flowing out of the bottom level or being pumped back
to the top to recirculate over waterfalls, shallow but
rushing rapids, cool dark ravines, winding slow streams,
or just overlapping basins of water that spill and splash
down one from the other. You can allow fish to swim
from one to the other, make narrow access to quiet
areas where the big ones can't chase the small or the
delicate-finned, or actually wire-off the approaches so as
to keep the fish separated completely. Not-very-difficult-
to-arrange-flexibility so that access can be changed at
will.

Whatever the shape, or the size, please don't forget

accessibility — someone will have to service the pond in due time and you will need to be able to get at all of it. Most difficult to service is the plain circle of the pond — all you can do is walk pathetically round the edge, reaching in some 60cm (2ft), and all the rest is lost in a desolate wilderness hopelessly out of reach. Who wants to wade into a stinking mess? Who can work efficiently in the swirls of mud thus provoked? Every tried catching a fish in such opaque 'waters'? Even one central 'island' would at least enable you to get a plank across, and work in between dread at falling in and impotent sulks at the stupidity of the pond design.

With the complete freedom of the exterior shape, subject to the choice of site as we shall discuss, goes certain basic laws governing the interior. The deepest part, we hope over one metre, does not necessarily have to be in the centre, though it will tend to attract to itself most of the mulm and other deposits and should not, therefore, be too isolated. If placed right on the unprotected edge, for instance, you might give a severe shock to the unsuspecting adult or child who walked in; yet it can be close to the edge with a separating shallowness or a protruding right-out-of-the-water motif or ledge. Sloping in a continuous line or stepping down in layers are well known and well tried; so long as there are provisions for housing plants at different depths, for example, the sloping line can have periodic indentations, or the ledges should be wide and deep enough.

Given the different depths which will be greatly appreciated by the fish and the plants, it might be useful to provide extra hide-outs and protection for fish from herons, cats, small boys and exceptionally prolonged cold or heat. An old piece of 10cm (4in) diameter drain-pipe will do fine, provided it is made of non-toxic material; the ends tend to get blocked so that it need not be in the deepest part, where most mulm seems to gather, and can even be raised-off the base by resting on some bricks. Also useful can be a three-sided box, closed at the top, and with an opening on only one side, again ensuring that the access is always clear, ready for an instant dash into the shelter. You may well find that your fish love these hide-outs resulting in the strongest staking a claim and keeping out all the others; it might be prudent to provide several!

Protection from the very real danger of grass-snakes will need to be made too. A rising wall at the pond edge will not only prevent excess soil from washing in with the rains but will help to keep out snakes, provided only that it is high enough, has a marked outward curve or reverse lip, and has no climbing plants growing up the sheer outer slope to function as neat scaling ladders for the snakes. Few country pond owners seem to realise just how many fish a medium-sized grass-snake can eat. This same wall will help to keep out much of the deadly poison of insecticides, fertilisers, fungicides and other unsuspected causes of fish deaths. One of the greatest of the bird enemies is the heron, which can clear most ponds at one go; however, it does not usually alight on water, and prefers to wade in, so that this wall may help if made wide enough.

Unfortunately other birds do alight on the water and, in infested areas, netting may have to be used. The new plastic types are resistant to water and do not rot quickly as a result of prolonged immersion; thus the netting can be virtually hidden by being a few centimetres below water surface. Thought for its anchorage either in the pond sides, or preferably hung from the protecting surround of the wall discussed above, should be given at the time of pond construction. The mesh of the net should be quite 5–10cm (2–4in) to allow the fish, and

and their fins, full and easy passage, not to mention growing plants. Equally the netting should be removable, in part or in whole, for later servicing of the pond.

An overflow pipe is most useful. The pond water surface daily gets oily, often gets covered with excess duckweed or other floating plants, and an overflow enables you to do a quick hose-off. A total drainage base plug is scarcely practicable, if only because of the muck that would be sucked-in to block it, not to mention fish and plants.

A few tips on making the concrete pond may not be out of place. When the hole has been excavated the soil must be rammed down till it's very firm; loose soil under a pond causes more cracks than anything else. Contours and sloping sides will crumble and give way unless reinforced and underpinned. This short paragraph accounts for a huge proportion of later unexpected troubles. As already stated the base concrete of a 3m × 60cm × 60cm (10ft × 2ft × 2ft) pond would be 30cm (12in) thick tapering to 12cm (5in) at the top, both being genuine and effective measurements.

Many concrete mixtures are advised, mostly depending on soil or climatic variations, but a reasonable one is 3:2:1, i.e. three parts of 2cm ($\frac{3}{4}$in) shingle, two parts of sharp sand, and one part of cement — all well mixed in the dry state before adding water. The prepared, firmly-bedded soil, should be well wetted, evenly, before starting to spread or pour the cement, to an adequate thickness and double-laced where stresses are expected. When hard enough the whole area should be re-surfaced with water-proof cement, at least to a depth of 0.7cm ($\frac{1}{4}$in), using, say, three parts of sand and one part of waterproofed cement. The smoother the surface the better. Both frost and sun can cause trouble during construction, not to mention rain.

The lime in a newly cemented pond can harm the fish, and many good preparations are sold to protect the water by painting on the separator before the pond is filled. Alternatively the lime can be drawn-out by adding to the water enough potassium permanganate to turn the pond from pink to red to purple, leaving for ten days then emptying and washing out before refilling and stocking.

Should cracks later appear, relatively small ones can be mended, provided further shifts of loose soil underneath don't cause more. Some people chisel out the crack into a 'V' so that a grip or purchase is given to the repairing cement applied to close the gap; the vibrations from the chisel have been known to cause other cracks elsewhere. The repairing cement should be quick-drying, a prompt cement, mixed with sand in equal parts; both it and the sand should be fine-grained to penetrate small cracks. Generally porous surfaces, over relatively wide areas (even the whole of the confounded pond!) should be wire-brushed down first and dried before commencing the resurfacing with waterproofed concrete.

Modern plastic waterproofers and hardeners are very useful for cracks up to one metre. Even the patented sealers sold by garages for sealing old leaking car radiators can help. A good home-made substitute is to get from the chemist some trichloroethylene and dissolve in it some old thin plastic oddments like the cups and saucers of the cheap throw-away variety. Inflammable and unpleasant to breathe, yet with care the resulting fluidic compound can be used effectively to seal most gaps, or even to paint considerable surface areas. All these compounds set hard very quickly indeed, and your skin will not appreciate direct contact with them. Some plastics are toxic, as the reader knows, but PVC, acrylic, etc., are harmless and are readily available;

the quantities used in proportion to the total volume of water are assumed to be very small.

Now comes the all-important question of siting the pond. Obviously, the higher the ground the better for the overflow pipe and for syphoning-out the water; much backache and elbow grease will be saved if the ground is high, or is artificially raised, so that there is a fall-away escape slope for the water. Then, how exposed is the site to the cold north winds, to frost, and to the sun; all three are of about equal importance in England. What protection can you give? Shade may well be helpful, but the leaves from overhanging trees are not; if there are enough fallen leaves then your pond can practically be guaranteed to kill fish and to go foul. If, weather permitting, the sun can be expected to shine on the pond most of the day, then green, smelly water can also be expected most of the time. This is the moment of truth, and has to be faced now. If your site has one of these limitations then you simply must build accordingly — against cold you need great depth, and one metre may not then be enough, or you should have a built-in heating unit; similarly against sun you will have to have running water, or at least a very easy flush-out system, or fit a really efficient filter — and that is expensive.

To make the best use of a site, we tend to face the shallowest end towards the sunniest spot in the changeable English climate. The excavated earth can usefully be piled-up at this shallow end to make an attractive rockery-cum-wind-shield, or front shield, or even shade-giver (in which case we like to plant tall, growing units, dense conifers, evergreens, etc., as will be discussed presently); the piled-up soil should be appropriately shaped and sited. Particularly it should slope down southwards to the water level so that the plants, including the marginal plants, are encouraged to grow. It will be on these thick plant bunches in shallow warm sunny edges that the fish will be encouraged to lay their eggs and where the newly-hatched fry will swim to hide. A protective wall, as already discussed, will help to keep out excess soil, fish enemies and fertilisers.

These shallow, warmed, well-lit waters are particularly rich in just the right infusoria and other microscopic life most likely to hasten and encourage growth of the fry; and, curiously enough, the adult fish either seem to leave these waters alone or they come there to sunbathe, basking in a lazy peaceful torpor, like we do on a hot sunny beach.

The rockery should be held in place with very large slabs and rocks, otherwise the soil and the plants will soon submerge them and reduce the total appearance to a heap of overgrown rubble. Rock pieces of 50kg (1cwt) each are by no means too large. Concrete slabs can be made to weather and mature more quickly by painting their surface with a mixture of manure and oatmeal, to which has been added diluted milk; this unappetising solution rapidly encourages the growth of algae, especially if watered daily.

Part of the best use of the site is to seek a pond shape, size and depth that will 'balance' that particular pond in that particular spot. The golden rules are the same as for balancing a fish tank, discussed earlier. For example, if exposure to sun is to be the main problem then lots of strongly-growing submerged plants will be needed — these do the photosynthesis job of giving-off oxygen and taking-in the bad carbon dioxide (see earlier) and further, these tough plants compete for the same food as the unwanted green algae, so helping to keep it down. Hence, your pond would need plenty of water, 30cm (12in), 38cm (15in), 46cm (18in) and 51cm (20in) deep

160

to encourage these submerged oxygenating plants and will have to be made accordingly. Furthermore, the wide-spreading leaves of the water lilies act as umbrellas against the sun, giving shade and cutting down on the light getting through; hence pockets 38cm (15in), 45cm (18in) and 60cm (24in) deep will need to be inter-spaced — these umbrellas giving shade here but not allowing light there where it strikes not empty water, to promote algae, but clumps of strong oxygenating sub-merged plants which keep it down as they thrive.

These lilies and plants will need to be strong-growing; that means they must be planted in rich loamy soil, but this is exactly what would also encourage the growth of the green algae we are trying to minimise — the problem is solved quite simply by leaving the base of the pond bare, but by rooting the plants individually in separate containers sunk into the pond at the chosen places. The added advantage is, that the pond remains clean, and is easier to clean. All manner of containers are available, from old wooden boxes to decorative plastics, just so long as they are large enough and porous enough to circulate water but not to allow the escape of the loam.

The exterior rockery of the excavated soil will also be arranged to throw shade, using conifers and evergreens, but not fallen leaves, as already suggested. Whatever the plants, they will need to be fairly resistant to industrial grime in cities and not to take on a dusty, bedraggled look too soon. Landscape gardening is a subject in itself, but varying shades of green, or tinted colours should be sought, in different styles and sizes. Many plants from the family *Chamaecyparis*, e.g. the blue-greyish-green pyramid of *C. Lawsoniana nana*, or *C. obtusa* var. *pygmaea* which is more flat-topped, with horizontal fan-like branches of bronze-green. Also

the junipers, the formal neatly-outlined grey-green
Juniperus simensis pfitzeriana, or the wide-spreading low
J. procumbens, or the plum coloured *J. horizontalis.*

Should the pond happen to be new, or recently cleaned-
out, the submerged plants and lilies will require time to
root and thrive; the green algae will be quicker off the
mark and green water may be the result. Hence it may
help initially to double-plant, deliberately putting in
more than will be used for the pond balance, having to
prune-off later. If algae really gets a hold, it, too, goes
on to thrive and to produce more advanced types of
algae like that stringy blue-green mass that engulfs
everything. Chemical inhibitors will keep it down, live
daphnia in swarms will eat it (if they are not themselves
first eaten by the fish), and you can drag-out much of
the stringy pest by twisting it round a many branched
twig swirled in a figure '8' or rotated under water —
done slowly most of the nuisance can be unwound from
the growing plants thereby saving them.

If running water is being used to combat algae, due
to excess sun, then the inlet and outlet clearly should be
at opposite ends. Further, the water from the inlet should
be sprayed or jet-thrown from a height to allow for the
prior escape of chlorine; splashing-it-off a (non-toxic)
rock or motif also helps. The same principle applies to
the flush-out system that may also have been incorporated. If a filter, internal or external, is being used, then
thought for its housing will affect the pond design; as a
basic guide, water is sucked-out from the deepest part
and returned to the furthest shallows. Worse than useless
is a filter that is too small or too quickly saturated or
too easily clogged.

Water pumps and fountains for garden ponds have
improved as much as have the aerators for fish tanks,
and many really good makes are available at popular

prices. Their help against algae is limited but they are certainly an asset against that other result of the sun — heat, especially sultry oppressive heat of thunderstorms. Most of these punps will lift a considerable 'head' of water so that really lovely waterfalls, cascades, rapids and sprays can be part of the pond. So, too, of course can under-water lighting be of many and of moving colours.

Still considering the best use of the site for the pond the problem of cold winds and frost are a nuisance for plants growing out of the water, like the marginal plants and the lilies. Screening can be effective against winds, especially if the piled-up rockery or other decorative screens are really close to the water, and can act for quite wide areas as deflectors. The problem of water freezing has now really been solved as heaters and thermostats are so inexpensive; all you need is access to electricity, if only a long waterproof lead back to the house.

Balancing the pond effectively means control of the number and size of the fish, of the plants, and of the dirty sediment. The rough old guide of a square foot of water surface for an inch of body size of fish still has meaning, except that a fountain pump adds 40% to fish capacity; recirculating water adds very much more, as the whole volume of water is brought into play rather than just the air surface. Regarding the pond plants, a rough guide would be your land garden — does it look bare, over-planted or about right? The same would do for the pond, dividing the total foliage between the submerged plants that do the real work but are not seen; the lilies that act as umbrellas; and the marginal plants in the shallows growing partly submerged and partly protruding-up to break water surface and reach for the sun, so attracting and encouraging insect life, thus indirectly helping the fish.

163

Excess sediment will encourage algae. As the reader has seen it is a good idea to plant in separated containers, easily removable, and leaving the pond base bare — although natural sediment and mulm will soon collect, unless kept down by a regular syphon-out. If the pond is left, neglected, then Mother Nature will impose her own balance in due time. Occasionally such a pond is sweet and clean when large enough; often it is green and smelly, especially if small, with algae rampant, to the extreme of blue-green coating everywhere — dreadful for the fish, and lethal to all the more-prized better-finned varieties. Such a neglected pond in its initial stages often goes green, and then clears itself, as the algae consumes the available food and dies. The crucial point has now been reached; if other plant life and fish are thriving, then the algae has been known to be

Fig. 24 Water lily

checked and a sweet clear balance results — though seldom without Man's intelligent help, for ponds smaller than 6m × 3m × 1m (20ft × 10ft × 3ft) — more usually the algae successfully competes for the food, overcomes plant opposition, and goes on to rule rampant. On rarer occasions the struggle goes back and forth as the pond turns green, clears, turns green again, clears, and then finally settles one way or the other. Chemicals inhibit the growth of the algae, but also of the plants; strong enough chemicals will kill all the algae, but also the plants — though not necessarily the fish.

Good, tough, submerged plants — strong oxygenators — are plentiful. *Elodea canadensis* or Anacharis as popularly known; *Elodea crispa* (larger, darker and more curly) particularly resistant to frost; *Elodea densa*, a giant variety but hates the cold; *Ceratophyllum demer-*

Fig. 25 Water mint

sum, Hornwort to most people, perennial but dies down to its roots in winter — a good asset as it leaves the pond 'free' when ice forms. *Potamogeton crispus* (bronze-green) and *Myriophyllum verticillatum* (delicate green

165

lace work) have the same characteristics of dying-down in the autumn to reappear in the spring.

Marginal plants that grow partly in 15—23cm (6—9in) of water, and partly out into the air are also readily available: *Iris pseudacoras*, or Water Iris growing 1m (3ft) tall; *Calla palustris*, or Marsh Marigold Kingcup, one of the earliest to flower, yellow and white varieties predominating; *Mentha aquatica*, or Water Mint, dark green, hardy and strong smelling; *Typha* species of bulrushes; and many others. If your pond is too deep for those marginals you could always artificially raise or suspend their containers.

Of lilies there are hundreds, literally hundreds, of known kinds, reds, pinks, yellows and whites mostly. Depth of the pond is the important factor, and the area available for spread of foliage — if the leaves are growing out into the air then the lily wants more room. Escarboucle is one such a wide-area-covering type, best in 46cm (18in) of water or more, and having a red bloom. Sirius, also red to pink blooms, requires less space and will also settle in 46—60cm (18—24in) depths, as does the similar James Brydin; whereas Froebeli is of a dwarf type flourishing in 30cm (12in) of water.

Supplementing the lilies for shade-giving properties are the floating plants like Water Cactus, or Water Soldier, with its pointed, prickly-edged leaves that tend to get frayed and bedraggled. Frogbit is a complete contrast of a mass of tiny floating, round, bright green leaves. Water Hyacinth with thick, heavy leaves and pods standing erect and proud, and the always-present Duckweed are two more contrasts.

No real attempt has been made to catalogue the many varieties of the four main groups of plants (submerged, marginal, lilies and floating) as your specialist dealer is certain to help and a balance between the four is really more important than fancy varieties — unless you become an enthusiast in this sphere and start accumulating catalogues and books!

Three very important aspects now need to be considered: feeding, spring and autumn. As the initial start to a good pond depends on its site, design and balance, so does its yearly health depend on these three new aspects. All three are inter-related, of course.

In spring the pond comes to life again after the winter hibernation of both the fish — and of the owner, who once again ventures out from his winter fireside to put a deck chair by the pond. Rather to his annoyance, the owner may notice that in spring the fish begin to fall sick or even die, because of the rigours of the winter just past. Next autumn the owner will have to take more care because that is when the real harm is done, although the results don't manifest till the following spring.

The ice and snow have finally gone, and frost beginning to alternate with sunshine the quick-growing algae and other lower forms of life seem to get off the mark first; plants still say dormant, and fish lethargic. Gradually the fish revive, and start swimming more persistently and searching for food; the owner's clue will come when the fish seldom revert to immobility and continually begin eating the algae on the pond sides, day after day. Picking a warm day for preference the owner should clean the pond. Old leaves, sediment, stringy algae should be scraped-out and removed; the water should be one-third or one-half changed, taking care to run-in the new water slowly over several hours, and allowing it to drop in a fine spray (or be jet-thrown upwards) from a height of 2m (6ft) — splashing it against a non-toxic rock will further help to dispel the chlorine gas.

167

This is now the time to start worrying your specialist dealer for new plants to replace those destroyed and to chivy him for live daphnia — partly as food for the fish

Fig. 26 Luronium natans

and partly to try and keep down the algae. You'll need plenty of daphnia. Spring is also the time to start feeding-up the fish again, and fattening foods are helpful in moderation, oatmeal for instance. Conditioning foods as they are called are available. Please don't overfeed in the early weeks or you will merely make more sediment and, therefore, more algae; little and often as the sun comes and the fish swim.

We always, always, feed in the same place, and, if possible, at the same time and in the same way, i.e. the same tap on the same stone, the same rattle of the tin, the same call of the voice, etc. Fish very quickly get to know, and the slow, the weak and the stupid have a chance to get into position beforehand. Even the slow owner has been known to take the hint as he finds all the fish assembled there — gaping at him.

As spring passes into summer and pond plant growth

and insect life thrive, there is an abundance of natural foods in the water and the need for artificial feeding decreases. If you are an enthusiast your interest will be more on spawning eggs and rearing fry, as earlier described; if not, you can more or less leave well alone if the pond is balanced, remembering only to turn on the fountain or to spray-in, from a height, new water, if sultry heavy weather persists.

Come autumn and your interests tend to wane, yet this is the real time of danger. Unless the pond base is clean, clear, especially of rotting leaves and sediment, with plants judiciouly pruned, with the water part-changed and sweet, you will have dead fish in the spring. Now is the time, sparingly, to feed-up and fatten-up your fish — just as you did the previous spring. Feeding only when the sun shines, allowing no unnecessary food droppings to encourage sediment and so foul the pond when the ice comes. As the fish go lethargic the feedings cease.

In winter itself the pond that was healthy in the autumn is likely to survive with the minimum of attention. Snow should be swept-off if possible as it blankets the ice and prevents 'breathing'. The ice itself can be left but two holes for air circulation are helpful; we do not advise sharp taps to break hard ice, as the vibration harms the fish and encourages the pond to crack. It is quite simple to stand a milk bottle full of hot water on the ice, which will neatly melt through.

Leaving the ice, with its two air circulating holes, it may help to syphon-off a couple of centimetres of water allowing that extra cushion of air to stay trapped below. In extreme cases the water may tend to foul, especially if excess sediment is present, and up to half the water can be changed, slowly, over several hours. It is even more important to eliminate the chlorine in the new water than it was in summer, as the new water temperature is low more splashing of the water is needed to dissipate it. Warm water should not be used, as it will wreak havoc with fish hibernation.

Water heaters and thermostats are readily available of course.

With any luck, all will be well and the miracle of newly-rising life that comes in the spring will delight you — once again.

CHAPTER TWENTY-ONE

MARINE FISH

With marine fish we are still in the good old days when no-one really knows, when no-one can commercially breed marine fish, and no-one can guarantee quantity deliveries months ahead as can be done for freshwater tropicals. Marines have long challenged us all; their sheer beauty makes them alluring, and in the 1970s they have crept more and more into our household tanks, difficulties not withstanding.

The real technical break-throughs are still to come. These are the days of experiments, of self-styled experts, of hopes rather than knowledge, of the thrill of the pioneer.

Yet, the golden rules are familiar in their broad outlines, being the same as for the freshwater cousins:

(a) how to reproduce a 'balanced' replica of the sea/coral/reef
(b) how to feed
(c) how to allow growth and cure ills.

Let's deal with them one at a time.

The ideal tank

At first, specialists all scooped up a bit of sand from the shore of the Pacific, the whiter the better; then they discovered that some sands were more porous than others, being composed of honey-combed oolites; next they found that some oolites were more conducive to forming algae and so they had algae oolites. They found some were lime-capped; some leaked silica; some calcium carbonate (argonite) which helped to 'buffer' the pH and gave stability, so that they crushed shells/corals to achieve this; or they wanted magnesium and phosphates, or other aids to beneficial nitrates (as distinct from the hostile nitrites); and they sought the balance by empirical trial and error. Most settled for a multi-layered base covering of three or more compounds, or of layers; what is used depended on supplies locally available and the persuasive sales-talk of the 'experts'.

But, all specialists know *what* they seek. A base that will rapidly mature so that beneficial micro-organisms overcome the hostile, one that will help make good the deficiencies of trace-elements, of vitamins, of minerals. In England many fell back, quite successfully, on three kinds of 'sand' plus the cheap (and porous) Westmorland stone. The whole secret was to encourage algae to grow in the tank *first*, before introducing livestock.

The depth of the filter bed need not exceed 5cm (2in), in spite of pundits who demand much more, provided the composition of the layers, and the air-flow through them maintains the balance — particularly with reference to the above named trace elements and to what is known as the 'oxygen tension' of the water, i.e. its cleanliness/richness/composition and its ability to support life.

However, if in doubt, then by all means increase the layers (or depth), but keep the water circulating through.

Meanwhile, the 'nitrate levels' were usefully checked with one of the very many aids widely sold, and the synthetic sea-salts used that more or less fulfilled their promise of 'instant ocean'. Since the stuff is not too cheap it is important to follow the instructions: 'The blunt fact is that ocean water varies as much as terrestrial water; not merely with locality, but with the seasons and temperature, with storms, earthquakes and man all lending a hand. Depth of water could also be noted.' Plankton is a constant missing factor; and Mother Nature's huge changes is the other; changes both rhythmic and spasmodic.

Mix the contents of your sea pack into 10–15 per cent less than the recommended water; if the tap water is already aged the specific gravity readings can be taken in 6 hours, otherwise in 24; stir well (not with metal!) and aerate heavily, stirring from time to time if the excess salt settles in the bottom of the container (no metal parts!). At last you can take the specific gravity readings (temperature correct?) adding tap water till the required reading of 1.025 at 24°C (75°F) is reached.

If this is to be stored, then darkness is preferred to light; before re-using why not filter and aerate it for a day, then introduce it to an aquarium.

Hints

(1) If in doubt about your sea water, heat it up to 60°C (140°F), cool and aerate; if cloudy, repeat the process.

(2) Specific gravity is normally 1.022–1.025, or even 1.028.

(3) pH (degree of acidity/alkalinity) is often 8.3, with variations from 8.1 to 8.5. Many gadgets will help you attain this, as also the DH (hardness of water).

(4) When in doubt, part change the tank water. Some do so regularly – the greater the fish population, the greater/more frequent the change e.g. 2.5cm (1in) of fish per 9 litres (2 gallons) of water could entail a 25 per cent water change every 4 weeks.

(5) Soak everything that goes into the tank in sea water (extra strong) first. The wise aquarist would previously have boiled the shell, coral, etc. after having

173

saturated it for 36-72 hours in a strong solution of bleach (3 cups to a bucket).

Smell everything that raises doubt. The human sense of smell is more effective than generally is thought; so check individually each piece of the tank decor, noting any 'softness' in the coral (scrape it away with a knife), any discoloured parts lodged inside (break it off/out/open with a hammer); note any patches of sand smudges or darkness (scoop or syphon clean); any tell-tale signs of decomposing fragments or dying crustaceans.

(6) If you can 'seed' your new tank with matured sand, that helps. As a substitute a pea-sized lump of crushed shrimp, for instance, can be allowed to rot in the tank till the smell clears in some five days; then the first livestock may gingerly be introduced if the nitrite readings are acceptably low (as shown on the colour chart of the gadget you have bought). Meanwhile, it is sincerely hoped, that algae growth is taking hold under the action of the extra-strong light.

Filtration

This is a must for marines; it should be strong enough, flow through the filter-bed thoroughly, and change through the filter media all the tank water at least once per hour, at least. Penny wise is pound (very) foolish. Ideally you should have a (strong!) under-gravel filter, plus aerator with a wooden diffuser, and (surging) power filter. It's expensive, but wise. Of course, there are many people who use less, or none; and they will tell you so loud and clear; however — you'll still do better to buy fewer fish and more filtration! Please do consider the enormous strengths of the surging/foaming/incessant currents that Mother Nature beats on her reefs of living coral; necessary to maintain the life cycles; and which we seek to reproduce in a fish tank. Once the marine tank is matured and settled the aeration can be turned down, but should be ever present to surge forth at the first sign of listlessness.

Why not incorporate a separate but linked chamber outside the tank on to which you can: (a) play extra-strong constant (day and night) light so as to encourage algae; or, (b) play your ozoniser so as to continuously disinfect the tank; or, (c) to provide an extra filter designed not so much to extract dirt but to inject vitamins/food substitutes, etc.? Many are the variations that a pioneer will try. Why not have several layers with varying functions in the outside chamber?

Ozoniser, Ultra-Violet Ray Tube, Urine Skimmer

These three gadgets, all expensive, are highly desirable aids and can repay their initial cost many times over if used with strong aeration. Unfortunately most aquarists find the price inhibiting, and hence learn the hard way.

The Ozoniser emits O_3 instead of the usual O_2 of oxygen, and can be used:

(1) to clean and sterilise very rapidly and efficiently (with the livestock removed) when turned on high;

(2) be kept at the more usual norm − 2−3 mg per 45 litres (10 gallons) − as a constant disinfectant, or used in fairly prolonged bursts at that low strength. Too strong, or too direct, and emission can harm or kill, and its reach is far flung.

Hence the complementary use of the ultra violet ray tube whose range is limited to the immediate vicinity. Play it on to the filter chamber, for instance, and no harm will come to the invertebrates like the anemones in the main tank, although water sterilisation will have been instant and thorough in the chosen area.

The urine skimmer came into its own as aquarists realised the ammonia compounds that resulted from

175

the urine (invisible in the water) were wreaking havoc with the nitrite level. An obvious sign of such distress caused to fish is redness of the gills, and/or accelerated breathing. This is important, and fluctuations in the rate of breathing should always be noted. If nothing else can be done immediately then at least some of the water should be changed.

Summary

Let us look at the tank cycle from another point of view. First, there should be provision for plankton, for microscopic floating life, from bacteria upwards — this should be encouraged by the inter-action of the base layers, the light, and the flow of the aeration.

The food chain of Mother Nature rises in a pyramid from this base, and gradually the plankton 'photosynthesises' (reacts with gases/organisms) to give larger and larger 'foods' in the chain links that nourish living corals, sponges, clams, scallops, tube worms, and the like.

Next comes greater specialisation and plant-stage growth like algae — both benthos whose threads cling to rocks, and plankton which free floats — with greater uses of light and vitamins plus salts and minerals to give the stable yet porous 'root' of coral rocks — 'live rocks' both moving and sessile (stationary). This is the stage of the marine invertebrates, e.g. anemones, shrimps, prawn and so forth. As this coral reef 'builds up', so is a home fit for fish formed. The whole skill is to maintain the broad based pyramid.

Hence the arguments as to where to place the emphasis (base, water, lesser life forms) and when/how it is 'safe' to introduce fish, and how many or how big.

Mother Nature tends to take back control if man fails. For example, you might arrange your tank decor to please your eye, only to find that the fish (and even the lesser forms) re-arrange/dig/furrow/transport so as to radically alter the layout.

Introducing and feeding the fish

It has taken thousands of years to establish the balance of the Pacific Ocean; man gets restless if he can't put the fish in his tank in two weeks. Yet the pyramid has to grow. One way of hastening is to seed the new sand base with culture from an established tank, and/or to endure the five day smell of a pea-sized piece of crushed prawn (or similar) — introduced as already stated. Another is to sacrifice a few hardy fish like Damsels to fertilise the sand base; the process first produces harmful nitrites, which gradually are overcome by beneficient nitrates. The aquarist hopes that in the transition of 5-14 days the Damsels will not suffer so much that they contract a disease like *Oodinium* as the copper sulphate needed to cure this disease inhibits the transitional removal of the ammonia and increases the nitrite poisoning of the water that had caused the disease in the first place.

Some aquarists remove the Damsels when they begin to suffer too much, and replace them with a relief group of fish — unfortunately this is not always practical.

The crucial period over, the nitrite reading low and constant, then permanent inhabitants can be housed. Some say, get the whole selection at once, so as to minimise later territorial fights; some say, keep to a shoal of small fish plus one (or even two) large; some say, never have two specimens of the same large fish or there will be fights; some say, always include a cleaner fish like the Cardinal; all are true, and are not.

Just try your common sense in avoiding disparity in size, in leaving fish enough room, in laying out your tank so that territories are more easily defined and respected and so that there are hiding places, free space, clear light, dim corners, thick layers of sand to burrow into — so that all reasonable provisions are made.

'New fish bring disease' to an established tank, perhaps because the new fish had the latent disease, or, far more likely, because the reduced space and oxygen left after the increased demand caused by the newcomer altered the tank balance and so activated the disease already present there.

And the fish to buy? The well-known ones, the cheaper and especially the smaller specimens, not the already large-grown: Angels, Sturgeons, Tangs, Butterfly, Bats and Triggers, for instance.

Really you will have to trust your dealer. And it's sincerely hoped that he is a *specialist*, and not just a pet-store man. So many other factors over which you have no control whatsoever outweigh the neat little text book guides, e.g. how were the wild fish caught? What drugs were used to stun them? How many days ago? What sort of transport and conditions have prevailed since? How many changes of water, with differing specific gravities, have they had on transfer from sea to shore to airport to shop to you?

For instance, earlier books used to lay great stress on floating the plastic bag containers to equalise the water temperature and to eliminate fluctuations of specific gravity; now we know that the microscopic pores of the plastic bag permit gas exchanges significantly to affect the fish and to make nonsense of the 'precautions'.

After all, these are pioneer days. The thrill is yours — as are the snags. No attempt is being made to catalogue fish names, as these change daily; each shipment bringing new varieties. Let's remember, they're all wild fish, few are yet commercially home bred.

Foods

To tempt the new fish to eat the land substitutes when just days ago they were free ranging in the ocean is a task. But, fish get hungry, they want to eat!

If the fish is 'shy' let the food lie still; if the fish is predatory let the food move (dance it on a thread/blow it with the aerator); smear a tempting spread on a piece of coral and drag it across very slowly; let the fish smell or, especially 'hear' the food; let the food fall in; don't let it stay and rot on the bottom. All this old-fashioned advice was/is true, and yet is not.

Newly hatched brine shrimps are often the best, especially if they have been able first to feed themselves in green algae waters; chopped white worms, shrimps, prawns, not forgetting greenstuffs like spinach, freshly frozen misus shrimp, frozen plankton (remember to sterilise the prawns, mussels, etc. beforehand by exposing them to the ozoniser or to the ultra-violet ray, failing that chill them in a fourfold strong dose of salt water for 3—6 days before warming and feeding) and, of course the many patented foods now specifically sold for marines.

Stubborn cases can be helped to overcome their fear (a protective cave, dimmed light, seclusion), to be encouraged by example (put them with fish that rush to eat); to be stimulated by vitamins being added to the water, by a $1°C$ ($2°F$) temperature rise; by green foods like algae rather than carnivorous fish or meats. To repeat, the fish *want* to eat.

Growing the fish/Curing their ills

Basically the same rules as described earlier in Chapters 14 and 15, including the variations of lighting, of floor covering, of diet that should periodically be varied — gradually and with restraint.

There are now sufficient patented medicines widely sold to meet most legitimate needs and the aquarist would do well to use them. Basically these fall into two groups: the spots-on-the-skin, white spot, type of disease like Oodinium cured by copper poisoning — 20 milligrams of copper sulphate per 4.5 litres (1 gallon) and the blotches-on-the-skin, fungus-like disease, cured by a composite dose of copper sulphate and streptomycin both at 25 milligrams per 4.5 litres (1 gallon). A variation of the latter attacks the gill plates and causes rapid breathing.

Much jargon is used to cover the fact that too little is yet known about the cures; dim light, increased aeration to restore tank balance, live foods, ozoniser/ultra violet ray, and urine skimmers probably do more in the end. Plus the good old 'change of water'.

Drastic but sometimes effective attempts with very sick fish — drop oil in its mouth or on a chosen part with an eye-dropper — have been known to work, sometimes!

But progress comes, and new medicines reach the shops. Marine fish are being bred in captivity, albeit spasmodically. Many an aquarist has kept a marine fish alive for years.

Let's hope you do too.

Index

181